Ezra Pound's Kensington

EZRA POUND'S KENSINGTON

An Exploration
1885–1913

———————❋———————

PATRICIA HUTCHINS

HENRY REGNERY COMPANY
CHICAGO ILLINOIS

Printed in Great Britain

Acknowledgments

The struggle here has been to keep a balance between the person, the period and the increasing complexity of Pound's work and contacts. I should be grateful for corrections and suggestions for further material when dealing with the later phases in England and abroad.

Many of those who knew Pound in London and elsewhere, or have studied his poetry and prose, have given much assistance with the present volume. To echo Pound in his introduction to *The Spirit of Romance*, if guilty of collusion they are in no way responsible for its faults.

First of all Ezra Pound must be thanked again for much material which otherwise would have been unobtainable and for permission to quote from published work; Dorothy Pound for her patience and care in answering questions, and Mary de Rachewiltz who gave her assistance on a number of occasions. Wallace Martin, N. Christoph de Nagy, William Rose and Noel Stock, read drafts and made valuable suggestions.

T. S. Eliot and his colleagues did much to help shape the final version. The staffs of the British Museum Reading Room and Colindale, and those of the Kensington Library, have been most co-operative, while the B.B.C. has permitted quotation from broadcasts. Messrs. Constable Ltd., Alvin Langdon Coburn, Erica Koch, James Laughlin, Vanni Scheiwiller, H. W. E. Lockyer, The Macmillan Co. of New York, and E. O. Hoppé, allowed the use of photographs. The executors of the estate of Ford Madox Ford must also be thanked for permission to use his work.

There is space here to list only some of the others who either talked to me or gave encouragement in other ways. Some must be thanked, if this is possible, posthumously:

The late Richard Aldington, Rachel Alexander, Agnes Bedford, Joseph Bard, D. G. Bridson, the late Phyllis Bottome, Rachel and William Cookson, the late Ashley Dukes, Clark

Acknowledgments

Emery, Ian Fletcher, Professor D. J. Gordon, the late F. S. Flint, Robert Greacen, Peggy Holdsworth, Elizabeth Haigh, Sam Hynes, David Clay Jenkins, Kate Lechmere, Margaret Morris, Lucy Masterman, H. T. Moore, Nest Elkin Mathews, Sir Compton Mackenzie, Sir Harold Nicolson, Jack O'Reilly, Jessie Orage, Hayter Preston, Brigit Patmore, Mrs. F. W. Philippe, Peter Russell, Allan Seaton, E. B. Scratten, Henry Simpson, Joan Stebbing, Millicent Stutchbury, the late William Carlos Williams, the late Harriet Shaw Weaver, Louis Wilkinson, Mrs. W. B. Yeats.

Contents

	INTRODUCTIONS	*page* 13
1	BACKGROUNDS—BRITISH AND AMERICAN	24
2	EUROPE—PROVENCE AND ITALY	37
3	LONDON, 1908	47
4	CHURCH WALK, KENSINGTON	66
5	SPIRIT OF ROMANCE	75
6	HOLLAND PARK AVENUE	88
7	CURSITOR STREET	102
8	DEFINITIONS	110
9	FRITH STREET	124
10	HOLLAND STREET	130
11	LONDON AND AWAY	138
12	INNOVATIONS	149
	POSTSCRIPT	159
	NOTES	161
	INDEX	171

Illustrations

———⊛———

Ezra Pound as a young man   *facing page* 58

Homer Pound   58

Ford Madox Ford, 1911   58

Ezra Pound, *c.* 1908   59

Kensington High Street and Library   59

Elkin Mathews   68

Number Ten Church Walk   69

Woburn Buildings   69

W. B. Yeats speaking his verse, 1909   106

Percy Wyndham Lewis   107

Ezra Pound by Alvin Langdon Coburn, 1913   150, 151

A map of Kensington W.8 appears on page 67

9

Illustrations

'Without strong tastes one
does not love, nor, therefore, exist.'

'No man knows enough about art.
I have seen young men with most brilliant
endowment who have failed to consider
the length of the journey.'

Ezra Pound

Ezra Loomis Pound was born in the mining village of Hailey, on the Big Wood River, in South Central Idaho, in the United States of America, on the thirtieth day of October, eighteen hundred and eighty-five.

Introductions

A good writer gives back what has been taken from a place or a particular atmosphere, if only in directing awareness towards its character and associations.

Although Ezra Pound's work always came from an experience, actual or literary, it was not topographical in the way that James Joyce made one city and a certain period the container of past and present, nor had he Henry James' concern with social milieu. Some creators,* not finding an early environment full enough, later identify themselves with another. Whistler, born in Massachusetts, painted the Thames as few Englishmen have done and the wide, deep movement of the river is there below much of Eliot's earlier poetry—indeed the inscape of *The Waste Land* may have also been an area in Hampshire.[1] It was he who spoke of Edgar Allan Poe as having 'a strong local flavour combined with unconscious universality', and doubted whether a poet or novelist 'can be universal without being local too'.[2]

At first this may seem odd coming from an author who, like Ezra Pound, has often been accused of having left his own country when it most needed men of letters. In their young days both poets escaped from conditions which seemed unsatisfactory and faced material and intellectual difficulties abroad. Thus they left themselves open to other cultures, indeed deliberately absorbed them. If Eliot was changed by the years in England, Pound seems always to have brought into whatever he was doing something of his early background. Yet in different ways each has returned to the familial as part of history. Having travelled through the ideas and actions of many other countries and phases, Pound has made full use of this in *The Cantos*. The universality in his work is conscious but it overlies an ineradicable Americanism.

* 'Artist' seems too limited a term now.

13

In Kensington Pound was *alive*—using his eyes. He noticed people on the way to post letters in that box in the wall of the barracks in Church Street, still with Edward VII on its red apron, or talked to the butcher about popular reading, listened to a remark from a passer by. Here and there throughout the immense compost-heap of contributions to journals in England and America, among the considerable correspondence, are sketches of his second most important environment, London before and during the first world war. Those were the years between twenty-three and thirty-five or so when he struggled to find his own 'address in time' and then, not unreasonably, expected others to acknowledge it.

It is often assumed that an achievement has been inevitable but reading behind the lines, it is clear that Pound's confidence in himself has never been complete; there were occasions when he experienced that cold key of disparagement down the back or the stomach cramp which takes every writer on occasion. Fortunately there was a quality there, something which has kept friends loyal to both work and personality, even when they disagreed with his views or met with disapproval of their own products. Without it there might have been no 'adjunct to the muses' diadem'.[3]

In writing about the past how easy it is to forget the every-dayness which contains events and to pump a balloon gas into another period. Looking over the parapet of Joyce's tower at Sandycove, perhaps the first to delineate his Dublin,* I had yet to come across Pound's remark about the difficulty of 'not being able to do a man justice without committing some sort of inflation'.[4] Yet a degree of magnification, even distortion is inevitable. It is impossible to work on a book without sympathy for those concerned, to try and place oneself back at a point where our present is unknown, Yet however flexible the imagination, there can be no re-creation of an entire atmosphere. The best an explorer can do within a taken territory is to examine the river-marks and rock-scratchings, the rubble and debris still about which can suggest, and suggest only, a previous era of consciousness.

Being as much interested in places as people, in practice I find a subject pushes itself forward, expanding out of the topo-

* *James Joyce's Dublin*, 1950. *James Joyce's World*, 1957.

graphical and historical layers of a particular background. There is also some personal line to follow, or the result is dryness. James Joyce, and Dublin itself, met a number of inherited but not always acknowledged resistances. A country where there are two hard-held dogmas and various political tensions, leaves few without the struggle to free themselves from it all. Some of the County Cork relatives, with a son at Trinity, may have been among those whom Joyce noticed in the drawing-rooms of Dublin hotels, as he made that prophecy in *A Portrait of the Artist as a Young Man*,[5] that another generation would seek awareness of his own people: 'how could he hit their conscience or how cast his shadow over the imagination of their daughters.'

Whereas Joyce meant an assessment of what was already prepared, in the end Pound obliges an examination of ideas acquired through education and the general ethos. If sometimes he may seem to be replacing one set of emphatic statements by another, it is often, as T. S. Eliot said of Pound's efforts as teacher and campaigner for poetry, as if he were 'trying to convey to a very deaf person the fact that the house is on fire'.[6] For one thing, I came to realise how much one's own youth was influenced by that 'privilege guilt' which had been in preparation several generations earlier.

To deal with James Joyce's world outside Ireland, it had been necessary to chart the movements of literature which were taking place during the second decade and to show how Ezra Pound helped to get his work published. I was tempted to land at interesting bays and inlets, to picnic with other topics by the way and once the main scheme was known, to continue with a search for sources. All the same, a rough map of the period spread itself out before me—the scholar would have thought it very sketchy indeed, and upon it were certain details concerning Pound's own development. If Joyce never really left his youth in Dublin, Pound was always moving towards the later years in Europe. He did not settle in England; London was no more than an important port of call, part of the 'periplum'.*

* A word derived from the Greek, meaning circumnavigation. 'Periplus also designates an account of a coasting voyage such as that of Hanno. Note, however, that Pound always writes of "periplum".' *Annotated Index . . .*

> '*periplum, not as land looks on a map
> but as sea bord seen by men sailing.*'

Canto LIX.

Introductions

The word suggests a return to that childhood experience of first being upon water, seeing the land move backwards, the familiar all different in its relationship of slope and contour because we are now upon the great, breathing body of the sea. Accepted proportions of size and shape, the individual's position in space, no longer appear final. Looking down at hand or foot, only the near seems valid and should the wind rise, even the balance and integration of the body become uncertain. Thus Pound, while using concreteness of detail in *The Cantos*, emphasises the shift and change through time of all but a few persistent values. Chief among these the Confucian concept of good government, both personal and public, a word again deriving from the sea.

If Ezra Pound happened to be in his room at number ten Church Walk, Kensington, on the afternoon of July 9th, 1910, he would have jumped up to shut the windows against the ringing of the bells of St. Mary Abbots' across the way. A chime cost several pounds my mother told me, when she and her sister had a double wedding there that day. A few years later, as children with a slight brogue, visiting London, we used to stop at the window of a toy-shop either in Church Walk or along Holland Street—anyway not far from the restaurant where Pound and his friends met for tea—none of our lives are lived separately. If some of the horribleness of trench and submarine warfare, the general atmosphere of England during the war, pervaded those early years, nothing could have been more remote from relatives in Addison Road or Earls Court than the doings of writers and artists living hardly a mile away.

The 'unkillable infants of the very poor'[7] in the tatters of Edwardian clothes, must have seemed different from the Irish country boys and girls who went to school barefoot. The frustrated young woman whom the poem describes as passing the railings in Kensington Gardens was surely some relation to those my mother, a widow by 1915, invited to stay at Ardnagashel in County Cork, so as to meet the officers in a convalescent home at Glengarriff.* Once when we were crossing

---

* There was a considerable heightening of the sexual tempo during those years, both a freeing from restrictions and a rather desperate 'catch whom you can'. Yet a 'lady' who had a child by an American officer was, to my knowledge, never forgiven by her relatives and the boy overshadowed by the 'disgrace' until his death in the second world war.

the Irish Sea there was a torpedo scare and another time we saw a zeppelin: after the peace, the gaiety of bands in the street was offset by the first sight of a mutilated man, hat held out for pennies. Thus one had known something of the same London as Pound—its smell of horses and cars, curtained houses with cedarwood boxes, conservatories, knife-cleaner powder, maids in white uniform, those bobbled mantelpieces loaded with curiosities, and after shopping, tea in the brown, steamy comfort of an A.B.C. Yet how to convey what had only been sensed from table-level as it were, the life of a generation adult before one's own?

Owing to 'the troubled times' and lack of funds, my education was very patchy. Much of what now seems to have been useful came from reading the great variety of books found at home. During the civil war and for some time afterwards, we went to various schools in Scotland and the south of England. Unable to go to a University, after several years in France, I began an intensive effort at self-instruction. Partly from curiosity, partly to please some young man or to keep up with new friends in London, one read T. S. Eliot's essays, understanding one sentence in four, and became interested in D. H. Lawrence, Aldous Huxley and some contemporary poets.

When *A Draft of XXX Cantos* by Ezra Pound appeared in 1933, I was again in Kensington, making good use of the library in the High Street which he had known earlier. The *Cantos* were not the best introduction to his work. The irregularly arranged lines, references to obscure texts, with American phrases thrown in, aroused a sense of persecution. It was as if a wall had been placed round what might have been an enjoyable area and the author refused the reader an entry. The reaction was not unique and occurs even to-day. In Ireland again, I met Desmond FitzGerald* and his family, who talked of knowing Pound at Rapallo, and then chanced on some of the translations. Later I heard a good reading of the first two Cantos; there was no escape. Pound was a necessary part of the 'paideuma'.†

* Desmond FitzGerald, 1889–1947, Irish poet, critic and Senator.

† 'To escape a word or a set of words loaded up with dead associations, Frobenius uses the term Paideuma for the tangle or complex of the inrooted ideas of any period. . . . The Paideuma is not the Zeitgeist. . . . I shall use Paideuma for the gristly roots of ideas that are in action.' *Guide to Kulchur*, p. 58.

Leo Frobenius, 1873–1938, German explorer and ethnologist. 'He came to be known as one of the world's greatest authorities on prehistoric art.' *Encyclopedia Britannica*, 1954.

In 1953 Pound, then in St. Elizabeth's Hospital, Washington (D.C.), gave permission to quote from unpublished letters to Joyce. I had moved after a decade in Dublin and was in Kensington again; through the kindness of the Reverend Charles Wright and his mother, it became possible to lease the house in Church Walk, Kensington, where Pound had stayed for a number of years. Thus we began to correspond:

'Don't run away with the idea that there was bad blood between Ford and Lewis/ they both had critical mind, an unusual command of their idiom/ Ford cert/ did what he cd/ to boost Lewis/

Jas J/ and W.L. together were more fun that a guignol, a pair of very cagey Kilkenny kats, or hyenas.

And W.L. must be credited with the: 'Don't see that he's got a very new IDEA about anything. Perfectly true but untimely, if one were putting over a masterpiece.'

The letter ends:

'/Where do you go from Jim? That enquiry perhaps premature.'[8]

At the time the thickets of *Finnegans Wake* had to be tackled, and I made no reply. When asked about people who had lived in the neighbourhood, Pound wrote:

'A map of Ken. W.8. wd/ be entertaining. How yu can get save *viva voce* from yrs/ anon/ gorNoze?
wasn't it Stendhal? who was it? Stendhal, Laforge? am utterly lost, but one of 'em did maps of exactly where
who at given moment.'[9]

Then one day in T. S. Eliot's small office at the top of a house in Russell Square with books everywhere among the furniture and on the floor, Lewis' angular impression of Pound watching from the wall—Virginia Woolf abstracted herself into the distance—the project for an exploration of Pound's years in London was discussed. From Washington the subject insisted the title should be in the possessive.

'hell NO!!!
my dear Patricia, NOT in "London". E.P.'s KENSINGTON, following Jim J's Dublin/ BUT much MORE because of fact.
Was not in London. months, possibly years never east of Cursitor St.

a few voyages on bus-tops to Southwark etc. BUT Ken-

Letter from Ezra Pound

18 Ag 57

ell   NO !!!
        my dear Patricia , NOT " in London " .   E.P's KENSINGTON.

ollowing Jim J Dublin/ BUT much MORE because of fact.

as not in London. months , possibly years never east of
ursitor St.

                a few voyages on bus-tops to Southark etc. HUH .BUT

ensington / stone by stone as Venice or Perugia /

hole point of its being a life/

y foot thru Ken.G. Hyde , to Mayfair and Soho //

eats'ever mournful ever weeping Paddington) Bloomsbury hostile.
            · another district.

hole point of map and house by house/ E.P's Kensington.

ny Sinclair emigrated but after having been geographicly Edward's
q.

ot Chelsea/ vid Tarr/ only for a few months had even. a visiting
oint in Chelsea.

roblem even re/ Hampstead, whether one cd/ take time and caHH
usfare to maintain relations. saw less of Rhys. after // approx 1913

ayfair , raids occasionally / or Mr Atheling's beat to
eolian and ²echstein (now Wigmore)   . •
            Pearya the baldheaded manager : yess, Vigmore iss
rench for Bechstein.

e may not have used that dialect. but e put a shade of intention
ato his irony.

sington/ stone by stone as Venice or Perugia/ whole point of
its being a life/

by foot thru Ken. G. [Gardens] Hyde [Park] to Mayfair and
Soho// Yeats' ever mournful ever weeping Paddington another
district/ Bloomsbury hostile.

whole point of map and house by house/ E.P.'s Kensington.'[10]

Mentioning the project to another correspondent he wrote:
'a life/ a MODUS, Habits, Modus vivendi; but cut the
"influence" cliché—'

At the risk of distending our title I have included a summary
of Pound's background in America, though he thought it rather
unnecessary. Without it we should only know half the man.

To understand the sequence 1885–1913, it has been necessary
to push forward through the work done afterwards by Pound
to reach the Cantos. There the Pound of middle and late age,
picks up sticks and straws, memories and impressions so as to
examine the details of his youth. His letters to friends and
fellow-writers have not been intended in the first place for publication and those addressed to number ten Church Walk were
chiefly notes and clues which I could follow up, with an occa-
sional aside or further explanation. By leaving these in their
rough state, with a minimum of typographical correction, they
serve to suggest how he would recollect a fact and then return
to it several letters, or sometimes a year or two afterwards, a
habit also seen in the Cantos. Whereas James Joyce drew much
of his material from reverie at night, or Proust used the early
morning imagination to recover the past, Pound seems concerned with full daylight, like a man talking to himself at mid-
day. Gradually one learns to listen and the fragmentary
associations come together as a known pattern.

At one time Pound wrote to me that he was 'still groping for
correspondence from Albion that showed some awareness of
the chronology, or as to the life of the MIND'.[11] I had come
across his remark that T. E. Hulme had declared that 'All that
a man ever thought would go on a half sheet of note paper. The
rest is application and elaboration.'[12] This was already in
Pound's books. Therefore it seemed best to ask for everyday
details, names of friends, reactions to other writers and events.
'In attempting to discover "where in a manner of speaking we

have got to".' Pound had written of Henry James and Ford Madox Ford, 'one can use allegory or data, trifling or grave things seen. The Goncourt insisted that the top belongs to reality as much the bottom.'[13]

The period has been allowed to speak for itself and Pound's own contributions used wherever possible. If the verse has been given little space it is, in most cases, available in the various collections. From books and talk, recollections and comments, an attempt has been made to bring together 'those salient details which are in accord with, or in a sort of complementary antithesis to the man as manifest in his work',[14] a phrase used by Pound when reviewing a book on John Synge.

While he was detained in Washington, Pound brought out collections of poems, essays and translations, and wrote further Cantos. Always considerable, his correspondence greatly increased. Every day over those thirteen years, in some part of the world, a postman delivered one of his characteristic communications. This might be addressed to a street in Belfast, where an admirer worked as a dispenser, another find its way to a Devonshire farm or a third reach a young man in Australia.

As we continued to discuss his years in Kensington, it looked as if this courageous man, however one regarded his views at the time, might well end his days in confinement. Neither his work nor his letters conveyed self-commiseration, but as groups on both sides of the Atlantic failed in their attempts to secure his release and yet another newspaper story dragged his name into disrepute, Pound must have experienced a further phase of despair, comparable to those which underlie the Hell and the Pisan Cantos. At one time his notes to me dropped through the letter-box at number ten Church Walk, perhaps twice a week. It was as though Pound feared that time—he was born in 1885 remember—might leave the record incomplete. In one of these, echoing another literary prisoner, Oscar Wilde, he wrote, 'I like biographic "fiche". In carcere one lives on postbag.'[15]

When *The Letters of Ezra Pound* appeared in 1950, no reproductions were included to show his highly original way of communicating facts and impressions. He is above all concerned with sound, with a tone of voice, accent or intonation, the speed of words in relation to meaning. In correspondence, as in poetry, the placing on the page is all important. Sometimes Pound used air-letters, written up, down and sideways, or single sheets of widely spaced lines, like shopping notes. Corrections or additions were in broad blue ink and when Pound was particularly pleased with details from London directories which I sent him, or research done at the British Museum, and maybe an account of seeing a friend, a Chinese signature was stamped in the corner. To receive his disapproval was to find a long, red-scored envelope on the breakfast table. A good cup of coffee and we could face it. There is little bite under his bluster.

'I took the trouble to send you a map of Kensington. Kensington 1908 to '20 could be pretty useful profile of the life of the literary part of the Brit. mind (when any) of that period . . . its too bad, because there is a magnificent subject/ AND plenty of documentation re/ a half forgotten epoch.'[16]

In the same letter:

'You can make KENS/ the centre of my activity, with forays into quite other London atmospheres. Hulme's dinner circle, and Fitzroy Street evenings/ different collection.'[16]

When there was a question of seeing one or two people abroad, he cautioned against taking on too much.

'Kensington wd make a book/ the continent an encyclopedia/ do eat in your dish which had a centre, until you lusted after the picturesque.'[17]

In spite of these advantages and the help of many of Pound's friends, it is not easy to write frankly of a man who can confront one with a repudiation. Yet sometimes a mistake can prove useful. On one occasion I had written in an article of the 'bitterness' with which Pound criticised the literary hierarchy in London, not knowing at the time that William Carlos Williams had done so long ago and received much the same reply.

'Do distinguish bitterness from DISGUST.

'I DECLINE to call it eau de rose. Am not bitter because there is dirt in a sewer.

DISSOCIATE ideas if you want to "write".'[18]

Later, working through his journalism of that period, one realised that he was right. Certain areas of the subject's experience—love-life and the rest—are cordoned off, though it is here that theorists will later disport themselves. On the other hand, many interpretations of events and attitudes can be in-

corporated 'for the record' and references to the Cantos suggested.

As Pound has been so long away from London and many of
his generation are 'to earth 'o'ergiven',[19] there has been little
vegetative growth of anecdote as in Joyce's case where his
books created a tangle of reactions among relatives and former
associates. Pound's later interests have alienated a few acquaintances and there is still much suspicion of his motives. Yet to
those who knew him during the Kensington years, as Harriet
Shaw Weaver said, with a little laugh in her voice, 'He was
always awfully nice'.

As this material grew, so we came to write of 'E.P.', as if
he were someone Pound had known intimately.

On the first of March 1957, he told me of a book published
recently:

' "Epoque 1900" by André Billy/ pub/ Tallandier Paris,
suggest you read it/ both for you and for me. You as model
of how to tell story of la vie lit/ IF there were any serious
criticism of literature, Billy distinguished lit/ and vie lit/
it could be used in my defence/

i.e. that from different angles/

E.P. 1917 wd/ seem to have come to pretty nearly the
same conclusions as old An. Bil in '56.

Strictly of 1885/ 1905/ few will now remember a lot of names
and associations/

a few mentions of W.B.Y. of interest to you also. A. Bil
[Billy's] ending up, that has told why a lot of rubbish shd/ be
pardoned and HOW it came to have been that sort.'[20]

When writing of that period and its tendencies Billy emphasised:

'*C'est de son désordre, c'est de ses contradictions, c'est de ses
générosités et de ses impudeurs, c'est de son amour passionné de la
vie et, en particulier, de son amour de l'amour. Car 1900 a beaucoup aimé. Il doit lui être beaucoup pardonné.*'[21]

'The essential thing in a poet' Pound had declared in 1915,
'is that he build us his world. . . .'[22]

P.H.
Autumn 1963

1

———— ✦ ————

Backgrounds—British and American

summary of Pound's childhood and youth begins with
a question. 'I dunno what my twenty-three infantile
years in America signify,' he wrote. 'I left as soon as
motion was autarchic.'[1] On another occasion, he declared himself to be landless, racially fifteen parts English and the re-
maining sixteenth part Celtic, born in a country where the
Anglo-Saxon stock was said to be in a minority. 'I am American
in so far as all my progenitors of whom I know anything whatsoever arrived in that country between 1630 and 1650; this
means that I am racially alien to the mass of the population in
the Central States of America, wherein I passed most of my
youth, for I take it that the mass of this population is either of
continental or of mixed origins. I was also brought up in a
district or city with which my forbears had no connection and
I am therefore accustomed to being alien in one place or other.
It is possibly easier for me to shake off certain prejudices than
for most men.'[2]

The name Pound has been traced back to the thirteenth century, deriving from those who looked after an enclosure for
stray cattle—not inappropriate considering Pound's care for the
pastureless poets—or a 'pounder', the maker or seller of pound
weights. According to a survey made in 1901, there were six
people with this surname in Philadelphia at that time, probably
Pound's relatives there.[3]

Later Pound was to joke about it. 'I am myself known as
Signore Sterlina to James Joyce's children, while the phonetic
translation of my name into Japanese is so indecorous that I am

seriously advised not to use it. lest it do me harm in Nippon. (Rendered back into our maternal speech it gives for its meaning "This picture of a phallus costs ten yen." There is no surety in shifting personal names from one idiom to another.')[4]

On one occasion when Pound was asked for details concerning his life he replied that an author's work was his autobiography, 'it is his first hand record'.[5] Running through both prose and verse are innumerable threads each of which can be pulled out and knitted into an arbitrary pattern—some incident or observation, a comment illustrating a general statement. An essay, *Indiscretions, or une revue de deux mondes,** provides a good deal of material about his early years but chronology has been disregarded and the easy conversational style leaves many queries. Pound in fact got tired of the subject.

'One offers one's little contribution etc. to knowledge and one stops (a) because there is something else one wants, more intensely, to do, and (b) because there are prosateurs ready to do this sort of record with more vigour and enthusiasm, and probably with more interest in prose than one has oneself.'[6]

Although he felt that the whole social history of the United States might be written from the annals of a family, Pound could not embark upon any such 'Balzacian endeavour' a remark echoed in a letter from St. Elizabeth's Hospital, three decades later, 'I haven't the physical energy to do the necessary 80 pages à la Balzac. At least nearer to Balzac than Proust.'[7]

In America the Pounds came from a Quaker family of New Jersey, some of whose ancestors were county judges 'and that like' in Upper New York State, others dealt in timber, horse-fodder, mines and agriculture. There was of course an Irishman or woman on the tree, who took part in the events of 1796, or maybe the later Sinn Fein risings. According to Pound, his paternal grandmother was 'of the family of Loomis, who were reputedly horse-thieves', and this is borne out by various books on the period.[8] When at college Pound met an old lady in Oneida County who said 'they were horse-thieves, charming

---

* *Indiscretions* was begun, probably in 1919, in Venice 'from a patent Italian inkwell designed to prevent satisfactory immersion of the pen. If the latter symbolism be obscure, the former is so obvious, at least to the writer, that only meticulous honesty and the multitude of affairs prevented him from committing it to paper before leaving London.'—Published in *The New Age* and various prose collections.

people, in fact, the "nicest" people in the county, but horse-thieves, very good horse-thieves, never, I think, brought to book'.[9]

Pound's grandfather, Thaddeus Coleman Pound (born in a log cabin in Ilk, Warren County, Pennsylvania, during the early eighteen-thirties), was a character of considerable energy and resourcefulness, who survived until 1914. He had known poverty but took to lumbering with success, ran a store in Wisconsin, built the first railway from Eau Claire to Chippewa Falls, from Abbotsford to St. Paul, and from Camp Douglas to Hudson, later extended to Superior.[10] By one of those extraordinary and often slow to emerge coincidences which research of this kind sometimes uncovers, Charles Norman in his book on Ezra Pound shows that in the eighteen-sixties one of the Gregory family of Coole Park, Galway, had been sent by Trinity College, Dublin, to write on economics in the United States, and gather information which might be useful in dealing with Irish problems. Horace Gregory, whose family were to be closely associated with W. B. Yeats and his friends, thus came to describe Pound's grandfather as a lumber-man 'quite notably distinguished among the public men of the great Valley of the Upper Mississippi'.[11] He became a member, and at one time speaker, of the State Assembly, delegate to the Republican National Convention in Philadelphia, and was three times elected to Congress. Pound maintained that he was rich before he took to politics and left them a poor man.

Thaddeus Pound seems to have had only two children, and his son Homer Loomis Pound, was to have gone into the army but changed his mind and worked in a Wisconsin store. When visiting New York he met some of the Westons, descended from stock which had not taken passage on the *Mayflower* but arrived decently on the *Lion* before the rush'. Through Joseph Wadsworth, who for some reason unexplained, stole the Connecticut Charter and hid it in 'Charter Oak', they were related to Henry Wadsworth Longfellow—which Pound does not seem to have mentioned much. The Westons were in business and the professions and Pound's grandfather, separated from his wife, had 'a sort of persistence in various forms of reaction, rather connected in the family mind with his "having ideas". He always had plenty of ideas.'[12]

When Homer Pound appeared from Wisconsin in an un-fashionable overcoat, the relatives of young Miss Weston were not very keen on her disappearing into the wilds of the Saw Tooth Range, five thousand feet above sea level. A portrait of 'Hermione', as she is called in the autobiographical essay, was included in *Pavannes and Divagations*, 1958, a young girl with a band round hair which may have given her son's its bright, springy quality. The conventional pose, with fichu and fan, suggests that she was only waiting to run away, and that her voice would be quick and incisive. Nor was she to be thwarted, for in due course she married Homer Pound and went to live in the first plastered house to be built in Hailey, Idaho, a place still very much on the frontier—with one street of wooden houses and forty-seven saloons, a hotel and a news-paper. The house is there now in what has become a town, con-cerned with trade, mining and livestock. Thaddeus Pound owned silver mines in the territory and he may have been instrumental in having his son Homer made Recorder of the Government Land Office where miners for many miles around came to file claims and have their ore assayed. Pound maintains that his father refused to carry a gun in case it would go off and hurt someone, and although he drank a certain amount of lemonade, gave no offence and was known to have attended a Christian Endeavour Convention. He was, Pound wrote, 'the naivest man who ever possessed sound sense', yet with a certain self-assurance, even sophistication.[12] 'The salt of the earth', he was to write, 'is not localised or monopolised in any one district; a suitable modus of intercourse occurs, regardless of national borders.' The three most moderate and rational people he had ever met were an Englishman who had travelled a good deal (perhaps Colonel Jackson of *The Cantos*) and an unnamed Frenchman, also an American [Homer Pound?] who had not been abroad until after his formative years. 'Not that they had opinions in common but the normal minutiae of their acts, their receptiveness, the considerations for their entourages were, as nearly as I can make out, identical.' Family men, they had escaped rigidity.[13]

His father often told the story of how at the time that Ezra was born in October 1885, the great elephant Samson broke loose from a travelling circus, upset the lion cages and chased the keeper out of his tent, while the cowboys pursued it down the line, letting off their six-shooters into its rear. When Mrs. Weston, his mother-in-law, arrived in Hailey, she exclaimed, 'Oh, Homer, how could you bring my daughter to such a place?' Then she could not lock her door at the hotel and Homer told his son later: 'Lock! Lock! You wouldn't, a man wouldn't, lock his door out there. If you locked your door, they'd suspicion you.'[14]

It is not clear if in choosing 'Ezra' for his son's Christian name Homer Pound was influenced by some family tradition or had an admiration for Ezra of the Old Testament, 'who mourned because of the transgressions of them that have been carried away'.[15] There is perhaps an echo of this in the title of *Lustra*, an offering for the sins of the whole people. Mr. Shandy found that 'there was a strange kind of magick basis, by which good or bad names . . . irresistibly impressed themselves upon our characters and conduct. One of those opinions which, after a free and unconstricted entrance into our mind—at length claim a kind of settlement there, working sometimes like yeast; but more generally after the manner of the gentle passion, beginning in jest, but ending in downright earnest.'[16]

The novelist Phyllis Bottome, who met Pound's parents in London, described them as 'a quiet old-fashioned and extremely pleasant type of American—common to our early childhood but less easily discerned now'.[17] Although her regard for Ezra was to retain its warmth until the present day, she always thought of him as an only child, given to having his own way. Perhaps it would be true to say that Ezra Pound, as he grew up, discovered that the world outside lacked that decency and good sense which prevailed at home, and he has always been trying to level it up?

Mrs. Pound found the high altitude of Idaho very trying and when her son was eighteen months old, took him to stay with the Westons at 24 East 47th Street, New York City. During the journey they were caught in the Great Blizzard of 1887, but fortunately the first rotary snow-plough was in use and its inventor on the train. The child was suffering from severe croup and the inventor, who has never been named in various accounts of the incident, suggested lumps of sugar dipped in kerosene.[18]

28

'And as Joel the brother of his great grandfather rode on the first railroad train in America, so the infant Gargantua rode behind the First Rotary Snow-plough.'[19] Pound was calling himself by the name used by Rabelais for a prince of great stature and appetite, who was also 'studious, athletic, good-humoured, and peace-loving'.[20]

This journey therefore provided one of those incidents—ideas in action—which had a particular significance for Pound. As he wrote, 'First connection with vorticist movement during the blizzard of '87 when I came East, having decided that the position of Hailey was not sufficiently central for my activities—came East behind the first rotary snow-plough, the inventor of which vortex saved me from croup by feeding me with lumps of sugar saturated with kerosene. . . . After that life gets too complicated to be treated coherently in a hurried epistle. It is very hard to compose on this topic.'[21]

Within sound of the bells of the Madison Avenue horse-cars, the infant Ezra Pound lay in his pram in the back garden while his uncle dangled from a window a strawberry on a piece of cotton to teach him to look about, 'to look up and be ready for the benefits of the gods'; and he spoke the English tongue, 'and used syntax and eschewed the muliebria of diminutives'.[22]

At three Ezra Pound was taken to his great grandfather's farm with the mansard roof in Wisconsin, and made himself a cane, imitating his grandfather, and spent as much time as possible in the large double kennel of the sheep dogs.

> *And the serpent appeared early in his garden:*
> *Venus in Sagittarius blazing near the midheaven.'*[22]

In 1889 Homer Pound, forsaking 'the vast possibilities of Wisconsin', became assistant assayer of the United States Mint, then in Jupiter Street and Chestnut Street Philadelphia, perhaps having learnt from mining-town experience what is nowadays taught in college and laboratory. The family first lived at 208 South 43rd Street and later moved to Wyncote Pennsylvania, a pleasant suburb. Their house, 166 Fernbrook Avenue in the Old York Road section, is still there, with its little verandah, and set among trees and gardens.[23] Of course there were visits to the relatives in New York and when writing of Henry James' *The American Scene*, Pound added a footnote about the earliest toy he could remember, perhaps when visiting a sick relative. 'I enjoy ascent as much as I loathe descent in an elevator. I do not mind the click of brass doors. I had indeed for my earliest toy, if I was not brought up in it, the rather slow and well-behaved elevator in a great and quietly-bright huge sanitorium. The height of high buildings, the chasm of New York were delectable.'[24] Later he declared that no English reader could know how well Henry James had described his New York and his New England, 'no one who does not see his [maternal] grandmother's friends in the pages of the American books'.[25] Mrs. Weston was a 'confirmed romantic' who read Scott's novel to her grandson at seven and told him about his forbears.[26] A monument of good sense 'à la New England', Pound said, 'she conserved more illusions, if indeed, romanticism be an illusion'.[26]

Pound remembered the classical frontage of the old Philadelphia Mint and how as a child he would pass through the weapon-decorated hall, salute the veterans smoking and talking, then stodge upstairs to the room where his father worked. There Homer Pound might be seated at an intriguing roller-top desk with twenty-three drawers, forty-seven slides and cubbyholes, containing a wonderful collection of oddments—stray lumps of gold, blank coin disks, photographs, religious and other periodicals, samples sent in by hopeful aspirants to fortune.[26]

At other times his father would be examining samples but his son was unable to explain why or how he knew the exact fineness of silver by squinting into one of the many cylindrical bottles. In these quiet rooms of the Mint the future writer was already interested in exact detail, training himself as assayer of a different kind, the metallurgy of words and ideas. 'The principle of gold assaying can be grasped by the normal mind. You weigh a sample of metal, you then place it on a cupel* of something looking like chalk; this is placed in an incredibly fiery furnace, and at a certain degree of fieryness the base elements are consumed or mopped up by the cupel. You then weigh the brilliant residue, and with certain repetitions, precisions, precautions, you know the fineness of the metallic mass. . . . The balances have tantrums in thundery weather. They will weigh you an eyelash . . . or a man's name on a visiting card.'[26]

Sometimes the lad went into the office where the 'boys'

* Small earthenware dish used in measuring gold content of ore.

worked, and once he was given a nickel by a Mr. Flynn but his mother insisted he should return the gift, to the surprise of that gentleman. She 'had somewhat that effect on the boys'.[26]

There is no record of Pound's early schooling but it was probably in the Wyncote neighbourhood. With the son of the Presbyterian minister, when ten or eleven, Ezra invented a djinn 'possessed of nearly all the divine qualities' so as to annoy a younger boy called Leidy who bored them by too frequently 'lending them his company'. For at least a year he was in the state of a man who calls for a priest on his deathbed; he couldn't make out 'if it was' or he couldn't 'be sure if it wasn't'. As Pound observed, 'enjoyment of this kind of hoax lasts into mature society so one has the news-getter and the fake litterateur who preserves these savage and puerile tendencies'.[27]

Pound's grandfather, Thaddeus, he was to declare, had fought the battle against injustice long before him.* 'The last time I saw the old man I must have been about twelve years of age. I can still see him, a-sitting in the so-called library at Wingate, in a big spring rocking-chair, facing a funny patent cast-iron grate, that was under my great grandma's picture. The other side of the family rather thought their side was superior; yes, being socially, etc., though I doubt it. I was great grandson, studying Greek, going to college. Well, so it happened I went abroad, and knew very little of him, till my Dad come on along over, and by chance, brought a few scrap books. There were cuttings about old political shindies, 1878, Grover Cleveland, and so on, and the swindle over the demonetization of silver. I could write a whole American history by implication, sticking to the unknown folks, in four or five families, but the war has been the same war.'[28]

There was also a great-uncle 'who had a wooden leg and went stepping around after Gettysburg' and 'wrote poems about General Grant which as a kid I did not understand.' He was probably the relative who said he preferred the Episcopal Church because it interfered neither with a man's politics nor with his religion.[28]

Pound had read standard fiction at a penny a time—Scott and Dumas. When reviewing Robert Frost's *A Boy's Will*, a memory of the country came to the surface. 'I was once canoeing and

* His initials and an account of the railway building occur in Canto XXII, p. 105.

thirsty and I put in to a shanty for water and found a man there
who had no water and gave me cold coffee instead. And he
didn't understand it, he was from a minor city and he "just set
there watchin' the river" and didn't "seem to want to go
back", and he didn't much care for anything else. And so I
presume he entered into Ananda. And I remember Joseph
Campbell telling me of meeting a man on a desolate waste of
bogs, and he said to him, "It's rather dull here," and the man
said, "Faith, ye can sit on a midden and dream stars." And that
is the essence of folk poetry with distinction between America
and Ireland.'[29]

This incident remained with Pound and found a place in the
Pisan Cantos:

> *The Pisan clouds are undoubtedly various*
> *and splendid as any I have seen since*
> *at Scudder's Falls on the Schuylkill*
> *by which stream I seem to recall a feller*
> *settin' in a rudimentary shack doin' nawthin'*
> *not fishin', just watchin' the water,*
> *a man of about forty-five.*[30]

'A fellow named Spencer,' Pound recollected, 'recited a long
passage of the *Iliad* to me, after tennis. That was worth more
than grammar when one was thirteen years old.'[31] This was H.
Spencer, Pound's instructor at the Cheltenham Military
Academy, Ogontz, Pennsylvania (1898).[32] Thus in Canto LXXX:

> *and it was old Spencer (H.) who first declaimed me the Odyssey*
> *with a head built like Bill Shephard's*
> *on the quais of what Siracusa?*
> > *or what tennis court*
> *near what pine trees?*[33]

Pound's family, who soon realised they had a writer throwing
the sticks out of the nest, treasured many scraps, among them
letters to Santa Claus, and some early poems. In a letter Pound
described 'the first attack of "style" or rush of critical sense to
the heart. At eighteen I always thought each poem the last.'[34]

Although Pound recollected that he had seen his father wearing a top hat, his impression was it usually found its way to the
box room.[35] Nor was it taken to Europe when he went there

for the first time with his son and visited His Majesty's Mint. There the atmosphere was highly formal and they were shown round by an official 'mainly concerned with his own lofty demeanour'.[36] There was Homer Pound, 'perfectly amiable, in a soft hat, accompanied by a lanky whey-faced youth of sixteen'. At home Ezra had been allowed to dodge about among the stamping presses or tried his strength on unliftable sacks of gold coin, amiably offered by one of the guardians with the remark, 'You can have it if you will carry it out.' And yet 'after eighteen years of reflection and a certain number of cosmo-politan contacts, I am still unable to see that that chap "had anything" "on" my progenitor—which does not in the least mean to say that I would not rather deal with six British Officials in any formal matter—say, passports, or something of that sort—than be subjected to one encounter with equivalent representatives of my own natal Republic.'[36]

Pound spent some years at Cheltenham High School in Elkins Park, and when not quite sixteen entered the University of Pennsylvania in the autumn term of 1901, under Arts and Science. First he lived at home and later seems to have been resident. There a fellow student told William Carlos Williams that he'd be interested in 'a guy in my sophomore class—Ezra Pound'. As Williams put it, before and after meeting Pound was 'like B.C. and A.D.'. He had a beautifully heavy head of blond hair of which he was tremendously proud. 'Leonine.* It was really very beautiful hair, wavy. And he held his head high. I wasn't impressed but I imagine the ladies were. He was not athletic, the opposite of all the boys I'd known. But he wasn't effeminate.'[37] Pound did a good deal of walking, played tennis well and took fencing lessons. During a weekend at Wyncote, Williams recalled they had a long discussion on subjects which William liked but had not had time to study, literature, the drama, classics and philosophy, these Pound declared were to be his life work. When Williams described Ezra to his mother, he was introducing that odd mixture of reactions which Pound was to meet throughout a lifetime. 'He is the essence of optimism and has a cast iron faith, that is something to admire. If he ever does get blue nobody knows it, so he is just the man

* Descriptions vary. Eyes, smoky grey blue.

for me. But not one person in a thousand likes him, and a great many people detest him and why? Because he is so darned full of conceits and affectation.'[38]

Ezra got on with that 'hard-headed English man who spoke right out', as Williams described his father. Mrs. Williams had a Puerto Rican background, was at an art school in Paris and seemed bewildered by life in a small New Jersey town. The young men talked frankly about sex. According to Williams, 'We were both too refined to enjoy a woman if we could get her, which was impossible. We were too timid to dare. We were in agony most of the time. Anyway, we survived with the loss of everything but our heads.'[39]

Williams noticed that Pound was always anxious to get other people started on jobs which needed doing. Long afterwards he published the translation of a Spanish story, done with his mother, from another of those books 'which Ezra Pound dropped into the house'.[39]

Williams, born in Rutherford Park, New Jersey, in 1883, was to practise as a doctor there for many years. He had been to Horace Mann High School in New York and with his brother spent a year in Europe before studying medicine. While working hard to qualify, there were times when he was tempted to devote himself wholly to writing.

'But it was money which finally decided me: I would continue medicine, for I was determined to be a poet; only medicine, a job I enjoyed, would make it possible for me to live and write as I wanted to. I would live: that first, and write, by God, as *I* wanted to, if it took me all eternity to accomplish my design. My furious wish was to be normal, undrunk, balanced in everything. I would marry (but not yet!) have children and still write, in fact, therefore to write. I would not court disease, live in the slums for the sake of art, give lice a holiday. I would not "die for art", but live for it, grimly, and work, work work . . .'[40]

Williams was to make a successful combination of both worlds, his search being 'for a knowledge of self, a realisation of his situation'.[40] While he was absorbing Keats and Whitman at college, Ezra Pound had already discovered W. B. Yeats. 'Ezra, even then, used to assault me (as he still does) for my lack of education and reading. He would say that I should become more acquainted with the differential calculus—like himself, of course, I'd reply that a course in comparative anatomy wouldn't at all harm him, if it came to that.'[40]

Although Pound was ready to joke about anything else he was 'always cryptic, unwavering and serious in his attitude towards writing'.[40] When he read his poems aloud it was almost impossible to follow him; such was his intensity that the lines tended to trail away. For Williams he was 'the liveliest, most intelligent and unexplainable thing I'd ever seen, and the most fun—except for his often painful self-consciousness and his coughing laugh'. Yet he could never 'take him on a steady diet. Never. He was often brilliant but an ass. But I never (so long as I kept away) got tired of him, or, for a fact ceased to love him. He had to be loved, even if he kicked you in the teeth for it (but that he never did); he looked as if he might, but he was, at heart, much too gentle, much too good a friend for that. And he had, at bottom, an inexhaustible patience, an infinite depth of human imagination and sympathy.'[40]

Williams describes how a group of friends would sometimes go to Pound's house for an evening, when Mrs. Pound, 'a remote, even bewildered woman, erect and rather beautiful in an indifferent middle-aged way, would play for us occasionally.'[40]

As a family the Pounds had always known good food and long afterwards Pound praised the old domestic standards which were already quitting American life. 'No second-rate cooking ever heated my face, till I got to eating in restaurants when going to college. And even then, God damn it, an oyster stew was an oyster stew. I mean as to cooking we were second to no man or woman of any station. French chefs were more fancy but ice cream was made of cream, all cream and peaches, solid peaches.'[41]

It seems as if the American young woman had a good deal more freedom than her English counterpart in those days, and was often on a more comradely basis. Among the students was Hilda Doolittle, later the poet H.D., daughter of a professor of astronomy, whom Williams describes as tall and blond, with gay blue eyes 'and at times a breathless impatience, almost silly unwillingness to come to the point'.[42] Like Ezra and many young people at that time, when the European tendencies of an earlier decade were still working their way through the American consciousness, she seems to have dramatised the part of writer, poet rather. According to one account, Pound gave her an engagement ring and asked her father if he might marry her, the reply being 'Why, you're nothing but a nomad!' for Pound had transferred his studies to Hamilton College at Clinton, New York.[43] The engagement, if such it was, petered out and as one observer in London remarked, 'I think Ezra had been keen on H.D. and then she was keen on him, you know the way it is.'[44]

Williams found it a bit annoying that he'd never let you in on his personal affairs. There was certainly some face, one face, which continued to shape itself before the young man's eyes, and here and there in the poems the suggestion of a disappointment, the clearest being the dedication of *Personae*: 'This Book is for Mary Moore of Trenton, if She Wants It.'

2

---⊛---

Europe—Provence and Italy

'Forgive the parents of my generation,' Pound wrote from St. Elizabeth's, 'poor dears didn't know any better. Thought they were buying us an Education.'[1] Pound had spent five years at universities and for the rest of his life was to speak out against the system as he saw it. An instance of what he considered the deadness of such institutions was the professor who discouraged his reading books outside the prescribed course. Yet he came across one or two men who made their subjects interesting, acknowledging debts 'to Professors MacDaniel and Child for Latin and English, and to Ames for doing his best when no professor of American history had got down to bedrock'.[2] Pound paid tribute on several occasions to Professor William Shepard, Professor of Romance Languages at Hamilton, who had studied at the Sorbonne, Grenoble and Heidelberg, and written on the medieval poets and philology. His instruction on Dante and the troubadours was found more important than any contemporary influences. This knowledge-able man helped to shape Pound's enthusiasm, though when asked about this period Pound wrote from St. Elizabeth's, 'I was NOT directed to Provençal. Shepard kindly gave me some when I asked for it.'[3]

Pound's first published poem appeared in the *Hamilton Literary Magazine*, 1905. Derived from an old fragment of Provençal, the rhymes suggest a movement towards one of the finest lyrics, *Langue d'Oc*, then technically a long way ahead of him.

Pound returned in 1905 for a further year at the University of Pennsylvania, where Professor Schelling, a scholar with whom Pound corresponded later, taught Romanics, and

Professor Weygandt conducted 'an odd sort of post-graduate course'.[4]

Pound received his Master of Arts degree in June 1906 and his father asked what were his plans. 'You've got to get busy and do something now, you know.' Pound replied with a poem, later printed in a small-town paper in Idaho—could it have been Hailey? There was a time in the lives of men when their fathers said gently that they could no longer stay at home.

> *'Twill come some time to you,*
> *When your noble Dad*
> *Your loving Dad*
> *Your dear Dad kind and true,*
> *Will no more pay*
> *In that generous way*
> *Your bills as he used to do* . . .[5]

During the vacation Pound was in Europe, and picked up on the Paris quais a copy of Andreas Divus' rendering of the *Odyssey* into Latin, an important find for him. He may also have been in London and visited Edinburgh; the spot at Holyrood Castle where Rizzio was murdered remained in his memory: 'How tiny the panelled room where they stabbed him/ In her lap, almost, La Stuarda/'.[6]

Pound obtained a George Leib Harrison Foundation Fellowship and went to Spain to do research on Lope de Vega. 'The general belief current during my youth at American beaneries was that one should go to Germany for systematised information. . . . I wasted time starting a study of Lope in Madrid.' On one occasion Pound told officials in the Bibliothèque Nationale in Paris that their book catalogue was a scandal. 'The idea was new to them. They fizzed quite vigorously and effervescently, but finally, seeing that I meant it, trailed off into eulogy on the larger appropriations made to keep up the British Museum.'[7] In Madrid he was allowed to use the royal library and is said to have been among the crowd outside the palace when an attempt was made to assassinate King Alfonso and his bride. 'For thirty-one years I have carried in my mind as a specious of rich diagram, the Prado as I saw it.' Pound wrote in *Guide to Kulchur*, 1939, 'In the great room, Las Hiladeras, the spinning girls, with the beamed light and the

duskiness; in the separate smaller room, Las Meninas.' There
is no space here to quote one of Pound's finest descriptive
passages. He sent back to a periodical in Philadelphia, a description of exploring Burgos and the background to a story of El
Cid. As in all Pound's work, the present was to inform the past
and a little black-eyed girl, who opened a gate leading into the
ruins above the town, became the child who warned the Spanish
hero of the king's wrath against the citizens should they
shelter him.[8]

Back in America Pound really had to get a job; his own
university does not seem to have offered him one. Thus he went
to teach French and Spanish at Wabash College, Crawfordsville, Indiana. Stranded in what he described as a most God-
forsaken area in the mid-west, the college library had proved
useless for his own work and he found solace in that provided
by the Carnegie Foundation.[9] Of course he was writing poetry,
and had told his father that before he died he wanted to write
one of the greatest poems ever written.[10] At Crawfordsville
he came across that atmosphere of dislike met several times
before. A colleague considered that there was much of the show-
man and the charlatan about him then—a superficially brilliant
and interesting man. For the authorities he was to prove 'too
much the Latin Quarter type'.[10]

Later the date 1907 was given to *In Durance*, stressing the inevitable isolation, 'Oh, I know that there are folk about me,
friendly faces,/

> *But I am homesick after my own kind . . .*
> *. . . that know and feel*
> *And have some breath for beauty and the arts.*
> *Aye, I am wishful for my kind of the spirit*
> *And I have none about me save in the shadows . . .*
> *. . . Beyond, beyond, beyond, there lies . . .*[11]

'If anyone shuts *you* up in Indiana for four months,' he wrote
to William Carlos Williams in 1908, 'and you don't at least
write some unconstrained something or other, I'd give up hope
for your salvation. Again, if you ever get degraded, branded
with infamy, etc., for feeding a person who needs food, you will
probably rise up and bless the present and sacred name of

Madame Grundy for all her holy hypocrisy. I am not getting bitter. I have been more blessed for my kindness and the few shekels cast on the water have come back ten fold and I have no fight with anybody.'[12]

After reading late one night, Pound went into town through a blizzard to mail a letter. 'On the streets he found a girl from a stranded burlesque show, penniless and hungry. The centennial history of the college records that he fed her and took her to his rooms where she spent the night in his bed and he on the floor of his study. Early in the morning he left for an eight o'clock class. The Misses Hall, from whom he rented the rooms, went up after his departure for the usual cleaning. They were maiden ladies in a small mid-western town and had let those rooms before only to an elderly professor. They telephoned the president of the college and several trustees; the affair became public, only one outcome was possible.'[12]

Another member of the staff declared, 'Gee! Wish I wuz fired!' and Pound concluded, 'Nothing like it to stir the blood and give a man a start in life.'[13] And that injustice, as it seemed to the young man, was to leave its dent. On the 8th February, 1958, Ezra Pound wrote from St. Elizabeth's, 'Must be fifty years to about a day, possibly exact, that I sailed from N.Y. toward Venice, my k-rear as a prof in the corn belt ended in smoak/ and DEEEspair of the future etc.'[14]

Yet the incident was not without its uses. Pound, who had wanted to leave America eventually, was now certain that his future was abroad. He travelled by cattle-boat and thus by the early spring of that year reached Gibraltar. He landed with $80 and some clothes.[15]

Ezra had first been abroad as a schoolboy in 1898, with a great-aunt who is 'Hebe' in the autobiographical essay, perhaps to suggest her good services, though the Pounds called her 'Aunt Frank'. This lady, presumably born a Weston, had met Pound's father before his marriage at some hotel in New York or in a more formal way, as part of the infusion of 'the unsorted heteroclite frontier life plus the wash of officialdom into the Jamesian atmosphere of New York'.[16] Yet although Henry James had described so much, there were many patches of undated atmosphere which had not been recorded. 'Why, for instance, my great-aunt should have danced at every "Inaugural" for a vast period of years, and why, having passed the span allotted this pleasure, she should have journeyed regularly to Washington to shake hands with the newly elected President . . . as regularly as she attended Dr. Parkhurst's or St. Bartholomew's on the Sabbath, or journeyed to Europe in June, with a vast collection of valises, suit-cases, hold-alls, hat-boxes and heterogeneous parcels' remained unknown.[16] There is a suggestion that she either ran an hotel or lost on it, as in Canto LXXXIV:

> *With that too large hotel*
> *but at least she saw damn all Europe*
> *and rode on that mule in Tangiers*
> *and in general had a run for her money.*[17]

Although his grandmother did not altogether approve of Aunt Frank, she had done a good deal for the education of her nieces and believing that travel broadened the mind, had proposed that Ezra should accompany her to Europe one summer.

Pound was filming a number of those impressions which he could always find again, having the faculty of quick recall. Many years later he wrote of 'a sense of man and of human dignity yet unobliterated. In 1906 in Tangier, you could see it in the walk of the Moslem.' Elsewhere he declared:

'Let it therefore stand written that I first saw the Queen of the Adriatic under the protection of that portentous person, my great aunt-in-law, in the thirteenth year of my age; and that my European inceptions had begun a few weeks earlier with the well-donkey at Carisbrooke Castle, Isle of Wight, and very large strawberries served with "Devonshire cream" at Cowes, and that the chances are I had "seen" Paris, Genoa, Rome, Naples, Florence, and probably the leaning towers of Bologna (these last from the train) in the interval. Or it is possible that I had not "seen" Paris, but Brussels, Cologne, Mainz, Nuremberg. The exact order of these impressions, seeing that I was to revisit half of them four years later, is now somewhat difficult to recall; and I do not know whether I have been twice, or been only once in Pisa.'[18]

Aunt Frank 'consented to admit that the one adjective, beautiful, was not universally applicable to all European phenomena, from Alps to San Marco and Titians (or even Murillos) and to the glass filagrees of Murano; but she continued to use it, with apologies. And her wide and white-bodiced figure, as for example perched on a very narrow mule in Tangiers, is an object of pious memory as she herself is of gratitude. Without her I might not have been here.'[18]

It may have been in Gibraltar earlier that Pound entered a synagogue and found himself included in the ritual, but it was probably in the spring of 1908 that he set out to find the background to Provençal poetry. 'Any study of European poetry is unsound if it does not commence with a study of that art in Provence,' he wrote.[19] To understand that part of our civilisation which is the art of verse, it was necessary to begin at the roots, which were medieval; the Renaissance, in turning back to the classical, had grafted its findings upon the changes which had taken place from the twelfth and thirteenth centuries. Scholars had long been aware of Dante's acknowledgements to his predecessors, and much had been made of the courts of love and their subsequent degeneration.[19] Pound, with his sure 'nose' for the untrampled, for the area where fresh wells might be dug and channelled down into the contemporary stream, realised that much terrain was to be re-explored with modern implements—the consciousness and techniques of expression accumulated during the intervening centuries. 'Any work of art which is not a beginning, an invention, a discovery, is of little importance,' Pound declared. 'The very name Troubadour means a "finder", one who discovers.'[20]

'If a man of our time be so crotchety as to wish emotional, as well as intellectual, acquaintance with an age so out of fashion as the twelfth century, he may try in several ways to attain it. He may read the songs themselves from old books, from the illuminated vellum, or he may try listening to the words with the music. . . .' Again [as Pound had done himself] 'a man may walk the hill roads and river roads from Limoges and Charente to Dordogne and Narbonne and learn a little, or more than a little, of what the country meant to the wandering singers; he may learn, or think he learns, why so many canzos open with speech of the weather, or why such a man made war on such and such castles.'

Pound's purpose was to suggest to the casual reader that the

Middle Ages did not exist in tapestry alone nor in the four-teenth-century romances, but that there was in Provence a life like our own: 'men were pressed for money; there was an un-speakable boredom in the castles', broken by this singing which in its time became an ennui.[21]

In and out of the verse and enriching the translations are images of the actual countryside, its rivers and hills and broken walls. The poem about Cino—'Passionate Cino, of the wrink-ling eyes/ Gay Cino, of quick laughter', has a sub-title, '*Italian Campagna* 1309, the open road', which suggests the air and sunlight known to both the fourteenth-century poet and his interpreter, who declares:

> *I will sing of the white birds*
> *In the blue waters of heaven,*
> *The clouds that are spray to its sea.*[22]

Provincia Deserta contains many images remembered from that first or subsequent visits, when the poet says:

> *I have walked there*
> *thinking of old days.*[23]

At Chalais he notices the arbour where old people sit, or creeping over rafters peers down at the Dronne, a stream full of lilies—one must not paraphrase so fine a poem; but just mention the garrulous man at the inn, the old woman glad to hear Arnaut's verse spoken, 'Glad to lend one dry clothing.' Thinking of the poets, and ladies, and feuds—

> *I have walked over these roads;*
> *I have thought of them living.*[23]

In Canto XX Pound relates how that year he went to see Professor Emil Lévy who had worked for long on the subject of Provençal and compiled a small Provençal-French dictionary.

> *And so I went up to Freiburg,*
> *And the vacation was just beginning,*
> *The students getting off for the summer,*
> *Freiburg im Breisgau,*
> *And everything clean, seeming clean, after Italy.*

And I went to old Lévy, and it was by then 6.30
in the evening, and he trailed half way across Freiburg
before dinner, to see the two strips of copy,
Arnaud's settant'ino R. superiore (Ambrosiano)
Not that I could sing him the music . . .[24]

'I know of at least one professor,' Pound remarked, 'who has produced a dictionary and remained delightfully human at the age of about sixty-five. His abridgement would have helped me to read the troubadours, if I had not learnt to read them before I found it.'[25]

Pound must have told how he had looked at the original manuscripts in the Bibliothèque Nationale in Paris and studied in the Ambrosian library in Milan, finding there the original poems and accounts of Sordello which differed from the version used by Browning. Long afterwards, in a phase of this exploration to be recounted later, I went to see where Pound had done some of this research, in that ancient building in Milan, deep-roofed and yellow as an old toadstool, cool and dark inside, one of the oldest libraries in Europe. A very ancient Praefecto courteously gave permission for me to be shown round. It was probably a long time since the name of Ezra Pound had been heard here and it drew no comment. Under the green glass lattices of a high window in what had then been the main reading-room, was a plaque showing that between 1907 and 1914, the future Pope Pius XI had supervised students there. Among them had been a young American with bright, upstanding hair. In Canto LXXX Pound wrote:

> *I knew but one Achilles in my time*
> *And he ended up in the Vatican.*[26] *

'First saw Venice in 1898,' Pound wrote in 1957, 'then 1902, then on escape from Wabash via Gibel Tara (I did not at that time, 1908, walk from Gib/ to Woptalia, nor have ever.) AND I can't take time out to detail grand tours pre hegeira/NO, H.J. [Henry James] did not draw my young steps to Europe/ I SAW Venice aetat 12 and returned.' When asked where he had stayed: 'Pilsen Manin [an inn], splendours of later era.

* Canto XXXVIII contains a reminder that James Joyce was educated by the Jesuit Fathers: '(and the Pope's manners were so like Mr. Joyce's,/got that way in the Vatican, weren't like that before).'

[In 1908] San Vio, over the bakery, by the bridge, possibly No. 631, then San Trovaso/ opposite the Squero, with magnif view down the Ogni Santi. 1861?'[27]

In 1919 Pound reflected, 'looking across the view of roof-tiles, sky-tones, mud-green tidal influx, cats perched like miniature stone lions on balconies' that 'Venice is, after all, an excellent place to come to from Crawfordsville, Indiana.'[28] From St. Elizabeth's he wrote, 'the Night Litany, preferable to some of the rest of it'.[29] In the poem of that name thanks is given:

> *For I have seen the*
> *Shadow of this thy Venice*
> *Floating upon the waters . . .* [30]

The Cantos, written much later, not only deal with the build-ing and the history of Venice but here and there suggest the way the atmosphere was absorbed during Pound's earlier sojourn.

> *And*
> *I came here in my young youth*
>   *and lay there under the crocodile*
> *By the column, looking East on the Friday,*
> *And I said: tomorrow I will lie on the South side*
> *And the day after, South West.*
> *And at night they sang in the gondolas*
> *And in the barche with lanthorns;*
> *The prows rose silver on silver*
>   *taking light in the darkness. ' Relaxetur!'*[31]

In Canto III there is a suggestion of regret again:

> *I sat on the Dogana steps*
> *For the gondolas cost too much, that year,*
> *And there were not 'those girls', there was one face.*[32]

Before he left America Pound had put together some of his poems, and even tried to get them published. Now there came a phase of dissatisfaction with his draft and sketch.

> *by the soap-smooth stone posts where San Vio*
> *meets with il Canal Grande*
> *between Salviati and the house that was of Don Carlos*

shd/ I chuck the lot into the tide-water?
le bozze 'A Lume Spento'/
and by the column of Todero
shd/ I shift to the other side
or wait 24 hours.

free then, therein the difference . . .[33]

Yet with Pound depression always resolved itself into action. It was not long before he was supervising the printing of these poems, on paper that had been left over from a history of the Church.[34]

3

---❋---

London, 1908

'And the U.S. thirty years ago was still a colony of London so far as culture was concerned . . . the only way I could educate the educatable minority in the United States was to come to London,'[1] Ezra Pound said nearly thirty-five years later. 'Henry James, Whitman and myself all had to come to London, to the metropolis, to the capital of the U.S. so far as art and letters and thought were concerned.'[2]

How far the stimulation of American awareness was Pound's direct concern on arrival in England in the autumn of 1908, aged twenty-three, it is now impossible to measure. He may even then have associated himself with Walt Whitman's sense of mission, but first there was his own reputation to make. It was a good idea to arrive in London with a book of poems, although published at his own expense and from such an unlikely place as Venice.

A note declared 'This Book was *La Fraisne* (The Ash Tree) dedicated to such as love this same beauty that I love, somewhat after mine own fashion' but as one of his first friends had died of consumption it became *A Lume Spento* (With Tapers Quenched) in memory of William Brooke Smith, 'Painter, Dreamer of Dreams'. The reference is to a passage in the *Purgatorio*, Canto III, lines 130-2, where Dante meets Manfredi, who died excommunicated and whose bones were carried with extinguished lights—without honours—out of the realm he was held to have usurped from the Church. Dante finds him among those spirits who were not destroyed by such curses and who, repenting, 'to the eternal Love may turn'. It is possible that William Brooke Smith died without what are called 'the consolations of religion'—yet presumably even so he would reach

47

Paradise. Later Pound wrote, 'I haven't replaced him and shan't and no longer hope to.'[3]

'I came to London with £3 knowing no one,' he wrote later,[4] and from St. Elizabeth's he told the present writer that he had a very small allowance from his father until 1911 or so.[5] Fortunately he did not have to put up with that, 'How much do you get paid for it?' attitude from his people. Perhaps an instalment was waiting for him in London for he wrote to Williams in October 1908, that his days 'of utter privation were over for a space'.[6] He also had an introduction or two, on this occasion or 1906 it is not clear, from Katherine Heyman, a noted American pianist, for whom he had done some publicity in Venice. She was 'naturally 15 years plus agée que moi' he wrote later, 'that was in "The States." I entered London more or less under her wing'.[7] A poem of 1908 dedicated to her and included in his first volume, contains the line: '*She 'twas that played him power at life's morn.*'[8]

Thus by the third week of October 1908, Pound was staying at Miss Withey's boarding-house, 8 Duchess Street, near the present site of the B.B.C. in Langham Place: this was 'the acme of comfort while it lasted'.[9]

William Carlos Williams had been one of the first to receive a copy of *A Lume Spento* and Pound wrote that he was glad to get some sincere criticism. Williams had found bitter, personal notes which Pound thought was due to reading in the wrong tone of voice. 'Is a painter's art crooked because he paints hunch-backs?' . . . 'To me the short so-called dramatic lyric . . . is the poetic part of a drama the rest of which (to me the prose part) is left to the reader's imagination or implied or set in a short note. I catch the character I happen to be interested in at the moment he interests me, usually a moment of song, self-analysis, or sudden understanding or revelation. And the rest of the play would bore me and presumably the reader. I paint my man as I *conceive* him, *Et voilà tout!*'[10]

What did Williams mean by 'ultimate attainments of poetry'? 'I, of course, am only at the first quarter-post in a marathon.' Of course they wouldn't agree, that would be too uninteresting. 'I don't know that I can make much of a list.

1) To paint the thing as I see it.
2) Beauty.

3) Freedom from didacticism.

4) It is only good manners if you repeat a few other men, to at least do it better or more briefly. Utter originality is of course out of the question.' . . .

'I don't try to write for the public. I can't. I haven't that kind of intelligence.'[10]

The neighbourhood of Langham Place was decidedly aristocratic: carriages and grooms, top-hats and furs just out from their naphtha, were to be seen in the sharp autumn weather. Cars, still with an upright-chair look, honked a way through the horse traffic of Nash's Regent Street. The red open-topped buses, with wooden seats and aprons for the wet, had not altogether replaced the older vehicles drawn by a heavy pair of horses. As an old shoe-black remarked to Ford Madox Ford, 'These are hard times we live in, sir. Now there ain't so many horse-buses there ain't so much mud on the streets, and it's bitter hard to get a living.'[11]

Always a great walker, Pound had to 'get a sense of a city like a savage hunter has the sense of the forest'.[12] He probably took short-cuts through the prosperous districts towards the British Museum.* There he found the Vienna Café where museum officials, readers and their friends dined, probably at long tables, the less well off having 'half portions'. Another time he watched people in a steamy ABC or explored the bookshops of Charing Cross Road. Everywhere Pound brought with him that curiosity which was to last a lifetime.

A few years previously, Ford Madox Ford, whom Pound was soon to meet, wrote of the currents moving below the surface of Edwardian England. Through the factories, at the docks, among the rich, or with an old woman making matchboxes, Ford recorded all with understanding. London was a

---

* According to the British Museum records Pound was first admitted temporarily, for one week, on July 2nd, 1906, and gave his address as 8 Duchess Street, Portland Place. The subject of his research appears to have been Lope de Vega and Spanish plays. On October 8th, 1908, he was admitted on a permanent basis, giving his address as 48 Langham Street, W., his subject being 'Latin Lyrists of the Renaissance.' His recommenders were Ann Withey of 8 Duchess Street, and Miss M. E. Granger Kerr of 38a Clanricarde Gardens, W. When renewing his ticket in 1909 his address was given as 10 Rowan Road, Hammersmith.

series of differing neighbourhoods, 'a gigantic tool-basket of a place'. The ideal writer of such a book 'should be passionately alive to life around him and yet be able to give a sense of all the dead Londons that have gone to producing this child of all ages, like a constant ground base beneath the higher notes of the present'. There was Trafalgar Square, 'with the glint of straw blown from horses' feeds, the shimmer of wheel marks in the wood pavement, the shine of bits of harness, the blaze of gold lettering along the house fronts'.[13]

By then bright and flameless lights had taken the place of the old petroleum lamps; undergrounds, once smelly and sulphurous, were now cool, white and brilliantly lit tunnels. Working people seemed cleaner; yet if living conditions were better, pockets of gloom remained. It was astonishing, Ford commented, how little literature had to show of the life of the poor. 'As we drive through the streets we see them in their knots, in their bands, at street corners; the parks are full of them, the public squares.'[14] Then remembering the last riots of the unemployed: 'We are the men whose hearts bleed for them but how, if they catch us on foot, shall we be able to escape from them?'[14]

Ford contrasted the way in which Londoners spent their leisure. 'Go down Piccadilly to Hyde Park Corner on a pleasant sunny day, on the right you will have all those clubs with all those lounging and luxuriating men. On the left is a stretch of green park, hidden and rendered hideous by recumbent forms. They lie like corpses, or soldiers in a stealthy attack, a great multitude of broken men and women, they too, eternally at leisure, dun-coloured, pitiful and horrible, two ends of the scale offered violently for inspection; the men in the windows never look down; the men in the park never look up.'[15]

For the well-to-do London was a pleasant place—plenty of servants, excellent craftsmen and varied entertainment. Ford, who was always pressed for money yet managed to go well-dressed into the social world, liked nothing better than to be in Piccadilly, five minutes after the theatres and music-halls had closed. If it had been raining earlier, 'The wet sides of the houses will gleam; the puddles of the roadway will throw up gleaming jets as carriage after carriage passes by, their sides too gleaming. The harness of the horses will gleam and the wet

Outside the theatres
at 11.15 P.m.

wind shields of the innumerable automobiles. . . . I will have upon my arm someone I like very much; so will all the others there.'[16]

When Pound had visited London in 1906, he had seen the failure there too and wrote later of his struggle to express this. 'I waited three years to find the words for *Piccadilly*; it is eight lines long and they tell me now it is "sentiment".'[17] Although the theme is 'ninety-ish', the scene was taken in with fresh eyes, and the poem, published in *Personae*, suggests the long road Pound was to travel to reach the austerity of the Cantos.

Piccadilly

Beautiful, tragical faces,
Ye that were whole, and are now so sunken;
And, O ye vile, you that might have been loved,
That are so sodden and drunken,
Who hath forgotten you?

O wistful, fragile faces, few out of many!

The gross, the coarse, the brazen.
God knows I cannot pity them, perhaps, as I should do,
But, oh ye delicate wistful faces,
*   Who hath forgotten you?*[18]

A summary of the period since the death of Oscar Wilde in 1900, maintained that decadence was now out of fashion, the manner of a clique. Though George Meredith had ceased to publish, Swinburne had completed another book, Thomas Hardy was turning more to the writing of poetry than prose. Joseph Conrad occasionally appeared in London. W. B. Yeats and George Moore were upon the scene. Arthur Symons, 'an exact appreciator of the arts', fostered the old traditions. Shaw was the leading dramatist, while one of the most able novelists was Maurice Hewlett. Mention is made later of Ford Madox Ford, 'a comparatively new writer', whose book on *The Pre-Raphael-ite Brotherhood* had appeared in 1907.

Yet Ford, who had been publishing novels since his teens, had written a number of other books. His father, Dr. Franz Hueffer, came from a German background of bankers and printers with relatives in France and elsewhere. A favourite pupil of Schopenhauer, a pronounced anglophile, Dr. Hueffer later settled in London and married the daughter of Ford Madox Brown, the successful Pre-Raphaelite painter, closely linked to the Rossetti family. He also became friendly with William Morris.

Dr. Hueffer did much to introduce Wagner and was for a period music critic to *The Times*. It is possible that while a student Pound came across his work, *The Troubadours, a History of Provençal Life and Literature in the Middle ages*, published in 1878. Ford declared that his father 'was far too much of an English gentleman to suggest that we should read his books— the famous one on the Troubadours, the other one about the Music of the Future and all the rest'.[20]

Later Ford Madox took the name of Ford, perhaps to avoid Germanic implications when these became unpopular, and certainly to the irritation of all future critics and literary historians. At one point Ford described himself as an Englishman with not more than a few drops of really English blood in his veins. 'The children of any Wallachian will become as English as the children of any Lincolnshire farmer,' he wrote in *The Spirit of the People*, 1907. 'The problem present always in the conscience of the American nation, is precisely that of producing a pure type. Without any secular traditions, without any homogeneity of climate, of soil or of occupation, the American has not yet been able to strike a national average.'

Dr. Hueffer kept his children in order, but had their affection and respect. The eldest son, Oliver, was given a good deal of attention, later becoming a successful novelist. Ford's sense of insecurity never really disappeared. Always 'they', those in authority, seemed to be assessing him. His father died when he was twelve, and their grandfather, Madox Brown, did much to help Mrs. Hueffer and family. Ford describes himself as brought up 'between the mighty legs of the robust Victorian poets' in a 'forcing house for geniuses'. At 120 Fitzroy Square, described by Thackeray in *The Newcomes*, as a child with long fair hair, dressed in a velvet suit, he would greet the visitors after dinner. On other evenings he used to sit on the other side of the rustling fire, listening to his grandfather and William Rossetti revive the splendid ghosts of the Pre-Raphaelites, and talk of Shelley, Browning, Mazzini and Napoleon III.[21]

Ford was not at a 'great public school' as he implied later, and to this day there are people who tell one how such pretensions were discovered to be untrue. Yet Ford had a good education and greatly benefited by the affection and culture of his mother and other relatives. At twenty-one he eloped with a young woman and settled in the country, writing a good deal. Then Ford met and collaborated with Joseph Conrad at a time when the Polish writer was hardly known.

According to H. G. Wells, Ford helped 'to "English" him and his idiom, threw remarkable lights on the English literary world for him, conversed interminably with him about the precise word and about perfection in writing'.[22] Ford himself believed that it was all one whether the artist were right or wrong as to his facts. His job was to stimulate enjoyment, promote discussion and awaken thought. At that time too much importance was given to fact finding. Accuracy of impression was all-important: his own business in life was to try and discern, to make people see where they stood in relation to their times.

Ford learnt a good deal about simplicity of style from a Scottish usher who introduced him to a wide range of authors, and showed how the sonorous, balanced Johnsonian sentence could be cut by half. It may have been through these influences and a natural sensitivity to language that Ford developed an easy, communicative manner which will weather many years to come.

Long afterwards Ford recorded another incident from his youth. When Dr. Hueffer remarked that Rossetti had written the thoughts of Dante in the language of Shakespeare, Ford had replied that he 'would have been far better employed if he had written the thoughts of Rossetti in the language of Victoria'.[23] His emphasis upon contemporary subject matter and clarity of expression was to be very valuable to Ezra Pound.

Such a *bon mot* about Rossetti may have been found later for Ford remained like one of those children who cannot tell the difference between reality and imagination, a tendency which seems to have increased. H. G. Wells mentioned that in the first decade Ford 'was very much on the rational side of life, his extraordinary drift towards self-dramatisation became conspicuous only later'.[24]

As Herbert Read observed, Ford had the modesty of the true artist, always dissatisfied with his work. He thought of himself as 'a bluff English squire but in reality he was very un-English . . . of German descent, blue-eyed and blond, thick necked and delightfully glutinous, he was typically German in appearance, and was 'without doubt the greatest liar of our time. He was not a malicious liar. I do not think he ever lied in a bad cause,' Read concludes. 'He had more absolute aesthetic zest for the art of writing than anyone else in his generation.'[25]

Meanwhile Ezra Pound had left Miss Withey's and found a cheaper room in Langham Street, next door to *The Yorkshire Grey*, kept by Mrs. Eleonor Joy.[26] According to a letter from St. Elizabeth's Hospital to the present writer, his new quarters were the 'seat of considerable activity', and he margins, 'burnt ms. of damn bad novel'.[27] He had told another correspondent that this was 'based more or less on experience', and 'I wrote myself into a state of exhaustion doing five chapters at one sitting, arose the next day, filled reams and then stuck.'[23]

Two poems of importance were written at Langham Street. In an article in the series *How I Began* for *T.P.'s Weekly*, Pound mentions those poems that arise from the emotional excitement of youth, when 'the subject has you, not you the subject'. Each poem had to be a new and strange adventure if it was worth recording at all. 'I know that for days the "Night Litany" seemed a thing so little my own that I could not bring myself to sign it.'[29] *The Goodly Fere* (Anglo-Saxon and Old English for 'mate', 'companion'), where Jesus is described by a fisherman, was a poem to bring Pound some rather embarrassing praise. 'Having written a poem about Christ,' Pound is supposed to have remarked, 'I had only to write similar ballads about James, Matthew, Mark and John and my fortune was made.'[30]

'I was not excited until some hours after I had written it. I had been the evening before in "The Turkish Coffee" café in Soho. I had been made very angry by a certain sort of cheap irreverence which was new to me. I had lain awake most of the night. I got up rather late in the morning and started for the British Museum with the first four lines in my head. I wrote the rest of the poem at a sitting on the left side of the Reading Room, with scarcely any erasures!' After lunch at the Vienna

Café, later in the afternoon, being unable to study, he 'peddled the poem about Fleet Street, for I began to realise that for the first time in my life, I had written something that "everyone could understand" and I wanted it to go to the people'.[31]

Only *The Evening Standard* even considered the poem, which appeared later in *The English Review*. 'My other "vigorous poem",' he continued, '*Sestina: Altaforte*, was also written in the British Museum.' Pound had had the Provençal poet Bertrans de Born on his mind, having found him untranslatable. 'Then it occurred to me that I might present him in this manner. I wanted the curious involution and recurrence of the Sestina. I knew more or less of the arrangement, I wrote the first strophe and then went to the British Museum to make sure of the right order of the permutations, for I was then living in Langham Street next to the "pub" and had hardly any books with me. I did the rest of the poem at a sitting. Technically it is one of my best, though a poem on such a theme [war; the clash of swords] could never be very important.'[31]

Among those Pound already knew in London was F. S. Flint, who had been introduced by another young man, T. E. Hulme. Unlike Hulme, he was without private means and had a job, also contributing poetry and criticism to various journals. At that time Pound had a good deal to learn from Flint's knowledge of French poetry.

'I remember Pound then,' Flint laughed. 'He had a tuppenny ha'penny sort of room, the bed taking up most of the space, beside it a *ruelle* in which he received his visitors. Ezra used to sit on the bed and recite Arnaut Daniel, which sounded like Bantu clicks.'[32]

There seems to have been much affectionate abuse between them, and although he appreciated the poetry, Flint never took Pound's enthusiasms very seriously. 'I mean to say, you take analytics—' he would begin. At one time Flint saw a very fine copy of Tacitus in Pound's room and asked if he could read it, and Pound replied, 'I hope so!' Odd the things people remember after so many years; Flint noticed that Pound's socks needed mending and as he lived at home suggested he should get them done, but no—Pound refused.[32]

Why Pound should move to Islington in north London about then remains unknown; nor is the sequence quite clear. He was to write of its long rows of depressing houses of grey-yellow brick as one of the architectural horrors of London. A later reminiscence belongs to this period. 'During the prelude of my London residence, before people began to let me into their drawing-rooms, I was permitted, even forced, to notice some of the viscera of this metaphorical heart . . . the implacable dullness of suburbia, often a healthy dullness . . . boarding houses, complete with billiard table (no cushions), bath, (out of order) h. and c. (geyser not working), pink, frilly paper decorations: complete board and lodging 12/6 per week. . . . Foods, unthinkable and unimaginable, odours, etc.! And I haven't been anywhere near the bottom. I've been far enough.'[33]

Again funds were short. At one time a young man of his acquaintance told Pound that he had the chance of a job in Paris but lacked the money to get there, and according to his story, Pound went and pawned some object and paid the fare. Characteristically Pound had forgotten the kindness however it was effected, and when reminded he remarked, 'only pawnbroking venture was in Islington'.[34] And further: 'When I raised 10 bob in Islington it was for personal use. Another ten bob was lent me, not at interest, by Miss Grainger-Kerr,* the Scotch champion of young British songwriters.'[35]

Curiously enough, F. S. Flint related how many years after Pound's brief sojourn there, he found a copy of *A Lume Spento* in a bookshop in Islington but unfortunately this was destroyed during world war two.

Perhaps Pound went to Brook Green near Hammersmith through Daphne Bishop (Mrs. Clifford Bax), who had a studio there and made jewellery, among other *objets d'art*; or he found a room on the suggestion of Ford Madox Ford, whose mother lived in that neighbourhood. 'Brook Green,' he wrote, 'and one at 3/6 per week but 3d bus [fare to British Museum] destroyed profit.'[36]

At first some people thought him rather a provincial cowboy and it was said slightingly that he was a postman's son: Hugh Kenner records the remark, 'A bore, and what is more, an American bore.'[37] Like Whistler and many another, Pound was

---

* Elizabeth Granger Kerr, contralto, b. Dundee 1864, d. London 1955. 'A very good friend of ours. . . . We were very fond of her.' Dorothy Pound to P.H., 1964.

not to find the American artist or intellectual much respected in London. Yet he was soon to make friendships among the discriminating, many of them to be lifelong.

One of Pound's immediate concerns was to distribute his first book of poems. As he remembered it, 'Saw London in 1898, 1902, 1906 and then in '08 arriving from Venezia with "A Lume Spento" printed, copies of which DEEPosited with Elkin Mathews and "Inigo" Lane, the two peaks of Parnassus.'[38]

At Elkin Mathews' bookshop in Vigo Street, writers who came to buy—or sometimes to sell their unwanted volumes—often met one another and stayed to talk. Mathews had been publishing verse for a number of years and brought new authors before a small but important public.

The firm of Elkin Mathews had published *The Yellow Book, The Book of the Rhymers' Club*, Yeats' *Wind among the Reeds* and work by many other poets, among them Lionel Johnson, Synge, Masefield and Newbolt—the list is long. Later it is possible that Pound, looking round the crowded shelves while Elkin Mathews was busy with someone else, might have pulled out a small volume published in 1907, called *Chamber Music*, by an Irish writer living in Trieste, but the name James Joyce meant nothing to him and it is unlikely that he was very interested in the poetry.

'It was not to be expected that a first book of poems by an unknown author in Venice, should attract much attention,' T. S. Eliot wrote about *A Lume Spento*, '*The Evening Standard* has the distinction of having noticed the volume.'[39]

'. . . wild and haunting stuff, absolutely poetic, original, imaginative, passionate and spiritual. Those who do not consider it crazy may well consider it inspired. Coming after the trite and decorous verse of most of our decorous poets, this poet seems like a minstrel of Provence at a suburban musical evening. The unseizable magic of poetry is in the queer paper volume, and words are no good in describing it.'

Scott James wrote in the *Daily News* that at first the work seemed 'mere madness and rhetoric' but later 'the curious metres of his seem to have a law and order of their own; the brute force of Mr Pound's imagination seems to impart some quality of infectious beauty to his words.'

Ezra Pound as a young man

Homer Pound

Ford Madox Ford, then Hueffer,
1911

Ezra Pound, c. 1908

Kensington High Street,
Library, early in the century

In December 1908 a hundred copies of *A Quinzaine for this Yule* was printed probably at Pound's expense, and a further issue published later by Elkin Mathews. The poems appear to have been dedicated to Katherine Heyman.*

Who entertained Pound that first Christmas? It is to be hoped that he did not, like Henry James, 'encounter three British Sundays in a row, a spectacle to strike terror into the stoutest heart, a Sunday and a Bank Holiday having joined hands with Christmas.'[40]

In the Vigo Street bookshop Pound had already come across Selwyn Image, Laurence Binyon and Victor Plarr and made 'permanent friendships' with them as he told the present writer, 'others acquaintances'.[41] Mathews sent him to Ernest Rhys, editor of *Everyman*, who introduced him to May Sinclair and she in turn presented him to Ford Madox Ford, then editing the *English Review*.

Earlier Elkin Mathews had lived in Bedford Park, Chiswick, where their only daughter used to be passed over the garden wall to be admired by a neighbour, John Butler Yeats, the painter, father of W. B. Yeats. Nest Elkin Mathews—the unusual name is of Welsh origin—remembers Pound visiting them when they lived at Russettings, Chorley Wood, in Hertfordshire, and how nice he was to her as a child—indeed he seemed very young himself, with 'high, copper-coloured hair'.[42]

Affectionately she quotes Punch's description of her father as 'monkish, mediaeval Mathews'. He loved his books and anything old. In that peaceful background which Mrs. Elkin Mathews created for him after the business side of life in London, books invaded every corner, even reaching the tool shed and the old harness room. Photographs taken about that period show Elkin Mathews at his desk, an ancient folio in hand, others suggest the low-ceilinged dining-room, with its brass Cromwellian bracket clock, the old oak dresser nearly covering one wall, filled with the china Mathews also collected. Several windows at Russettings overlooked the woods and to hear Miss Elkin Mathews describe the place gives an idea of the pleasant atmosphere Pound encountered there.

* See *A Bibliography of Ezra Pound*, Donald Gallup, 1963, for the history of volumes or poems mentioned here.

Pound has several times mentioned 'that touching little scene in Elkin Mathews' shop' concerning his poems:

'Mathews: "Ah, eh, ah, would you, now, be prepared to assist in the publication?"'

'E.P.: "I've a shilling in my clothes, if that's any use to you?"'

'Mathews: "Oh well, I want to publish 'em. Anyhow."'

'And he did.'[43]

Thus by 3rd February, 1909, Pound was telling Williams 'Am by way of falling into the crowd that does things here. London, deah old Lundon, is the place for poesy. . . . If you have saved any pennies during your stay in Nueva York, you'd better come across and broaden your mind.'[44] Mathews was soon to publish *Personae*, a title derived from the masks used by actors in ancient plays to assume different personalities; what was more, Pound was to get the same terms as Maurice Hewlett, the well-known novelist.

As Ezra Pound wrote to Mrs. Mathews in 1922, 'Whatever has been done since, I shall not forget that he was the first who accepted my work when I landed in London—sans sous—and these beginnings count for more than the middle steps of the journey.'[45]

Ford was always talking about the great men he had met, among them Algernon Swinburne. Pound, who had written a poem to Swinburne, when he was twenty-one—balderdash he called it later—considered him and Browning the best poets of the Victorian era. He may have hoped it would be possible for Ford or someone else to take him along to The Pines, an upright semi-detached villa still to be seen at the foot of Putney Hill. There Swinburne lived with the solicitor Watts-Dunton, introduced by Ford Madox Brown, whom some, according to their reception there, called guardian or friend of the poet, others his keeper. In his prose and also in the Cantos Pound mentioned a number of anecdotes.

> *Swinburne my only miss*
> *and I didn't know he'd been to see Landor*
>   *and they told me this that an' t'other*
>
> *and when old Mathews went he saw the three teacups*
>   *two for Watts Dunton who liked to let his tea cool,*

So old Elkin had only one glory
He did carry Algernon's suit case once
when he, Elkin, first came to London.[46]

Mathews would have been middle-aged at the time *—which seemed ancient to the young American. 'We're finished at forty!' he gaily told Phyllis Bottome—a notion rescinded later.[47]

In the November following Pound's arrival in London, Swinburne caught a chill from going across Putney Common without his overcoat, and this became pneumonia, but he recovered. Then early in the spring of 1909 several members of the household at The Pines caught 'flu and on April 10 Swinburne died. As a schoolboy he had seen Wordsworth, later dined with Tennyson, known Dickens, Victor Hugo, all the Pre-Raphaelites, encountered disapproval and been given great praise. As Ford wrote in *The English Review* when George Meredith died in May 1909, 'Now indeed, the whole Round Table is demolished . . . with the last great figure of the Victorian group that in its literature and its culture was so dominated by the Arthurian cycle. . . . And like Mr Swinburne, Mr Meredith has not been buried in the Abbey.'

Hardly a week after Swinburne's death, Pound's second volume of poems, *Personae*, appeared, the first of many to be published in England, and this can now be seen as the beginning of a new period in English and American literature.

In those days London had a great number of clubs. Beside the hardy annuals of Pall Mall and St. James' there was a number of less rooted growth, some rising quickly and dying away again. These seldom had premises, their members meeting every so often for dinner at a restaurant, evening dress usually being worn. On the other hand, according to Edgar Jepson, there was no need of a dinner jacket at 'The Square', because 'they were not worn in garden cities'. Founded by G. K. Chesterton and another, to honour Fielding, it included among its members Walter de la Mare, John Masefield, Galsworthy and H. W. Nevinson of the *Daily News*. Ford Madox Ford was quite often there, 'talking little but listening and surveying the literary friends of his callow youth with a sinister and mocking wariness'.[48]

* Elkin Mathews, 1851–1921.

It was at 'The Square' that Jepson first met Ezra Pound, whom he was occasionally to encounter elsewhere, 'crowned with a mass of bright fair hair and often bearded; wearing a velvet coat and one turquoise ear-ring, he was the most picturesque of the Pennsylvanians, and how the so much dingier Square Club writers did hate that picturesqueness! I always saw him, not so much as a poet, as the warrior of the arts and the vigour and enthusiasm with which he waged his battles against the pudwiggens of the academic and literary traditions were as valuable as they were immense.' Jepson often found it tiresome to listen to Pound discussing his theories in an earnest whisper after the manner of Ford. Women, this shrewd observer remarked, 'ran after him with commendable pertinacity'.[48]

The critics of the Square Club had a damping effect on other members. 'You could not be a poet in those days unless they discovered and made you.' Then Edward Thomas 'fairly tore it'; in *The English Review*, June 1909; '*he praised* the verse of Ezra Pound'. Recognizing the first-hand intensity of feeling and the book's 'vague, large promise' he foresaw 'that battle with the world of a fresh soul who feels himself strong but alone, and the battle with words, the beautiful, the soiled, the rare, the antique words'. There was none of the surface qualities of contemporary verse nor the melancholy, resignation or unwillingness to live, but an element of truth to himself; he was full of personality and the power to express it, 'from the first to the last lines of most of his poems he holds us steadily in his own pure, grave, passionate world'.

'I shall never forget the meeting of the "Square Club" a few days after that monstrous action,' Jepson wrote. 'The pale, shocked, contorted glances of the poet-makers . . . the nervous leaping into corners; the shocked whispers, the jerky gestures; even between courses the hard sound of grinding teeth. Poor Edward Thomas! He did look so hot and bothered. . . . How could he have liked the verse of a man whom none of them had discovered, much less made! The Club rocked to its Foundations and so did English literature!'[48]

F. S. Flint, reviewing *Personae* in *The New Age*, May 1909, found that 'Mr Pound is a poet with a distinct personality. Essentially he is a rebel against all conventions except sanity: there is something robustly impish and elfish about him. He

writes with fresh beauty and vigour. This book is tufted with
beauty as the bole of an old elm tree with green shoots.'[49]

In the poem *The White Stag*, as Flint noted, 'perhaps Pound
was himself among those who he saw 'coursing and crying',

> '*Tis the white stag, Fame, we're a-hunting,*
> *Bid the world's hounds come to horn!'*[50]

In May Pound was writing to William Carlos Williams, 'I
have sinned in nearly every possible way, even the ways I most
condemn. I have printed too much. I have been praised by
[W. B. Yeats] the greatest living poet. I am, after eight years'
hammering against the impenetrable adamant, become suddenly somewhat of a success. . . . There is no town like London
to make one feel the vanity of all art except the highest. To
make one disbelieve in all but the most careful and conservative
presentation of one's stuff. I have sinned deeply against the
doctrine I preach.'[51]

Pound suggests Williams should read Yeats, Browning and
Francis Thompson, Swinburne and Rossetti to learn something
of the progress of English poetry in the past century. A number of people of second rank were doing 'damn good work'.
Williams was out of touch; that was all. 'Learn your art
thoroughly,' he advises. Then as a postscript, applicable to
both young men. 'And remember a man's real work is what *he
is going to do*, not what is behind him. Avanti e coraggio!'[51]

There is a copy of *Personae* at the British Museum, stamped
as received on 16 April 1909, a little book of dark grey boards,
broken at the edges now, the gold lettering softened down from
its original brightness. On the fly leaf is an unacknowledged
quotation, *Make strong old dreams lest this our world lose heart*,
and the tentative dedication to the American girl whom Pound
was not to forget.

In the course of the first poem, *Grace before Song*, the poet
declares:

> *As bright white drops upon a leaden sea,*
> *Grant so my songs to this grey folk may be;*
> *As drops that dream and gleam and falling catch*
> *   the sun,*
> *Evanescent mirrors every opal one . . .* *

* This poem introduced *A Lume Spento* and *Umbra*, 1920

The image evidently struck Virginia Woolf as original for she used it when writing of Oliver Wendell Holmes in the *Times Literary Supplement* that August.

A hundred years ago it had been easier to talk of a distinctive American contribution to literature, but with increasing coming and going across the Atlantic, 'Save for the voice and certain small differences of manner which gives them a flavour of their own, Americans sink into us, over here, like raindrops into the sea.' They had lost much of the nervous desire to assert their own independence or maturity, 'in opposition to a mother country which was always reminding them of their tender age'. Yet to understand American art and politics, 'we must look as closely as when blood and speech are strange to us.' Intimacy should be based on an understanding that we differ in many ways. Virginia Woolf also noted the typical American defect of over-ingenuity, 'and an uneasy love of decoration as though they had not yet learnt the art of sitting still.'[52]

Although much of Pound's work at that time—he was twenty-four in 1909—contains reminders of the poetry absorbed over a decade, perhaps Virginia Woolf may have sensed there the search for an expression of this difference. Of course she could not foresee that such showers of rain would later reach gale force and blow away a great many temporary shacks and shanties.

In the first edition of *Personae*, a title Pound was also to use for a later collection, there is a stage direction to the poem *La Fraisne*; 'Scene: the Ash Wood, near Malvern,' which was dropped subsequently. If this is a reference to an English region, presumably the poem was drafted, or actually written, when Pound was in England in 1906. During the first five years, he related, 'I had exactly one brief poem accepted by one American magazine, although I had during that time submitted *La Fraisne* and various other poems now held to be part of my best work. Net result of my activities in cash, five dollars which works out to about 4/3 per year.'[53] The theme is that of the Provençal poet who from the love of a lady, ran mad in the forest to find there a greater love:

> *That is sweeter than the love of women*
> *That plague and burn and drive one away.*[54]

A note at the back of the volume, suggests that it arose not only from Pound's study of the early poets, but as so often in his work, from an intense personal experience. He quotes Janus of Basel on the spirit returning to its primal nature and finding peace, and continues in rather high-flown prose.

'Also has Mr Yeats in his *Celtic Twilight* treated of such, and I because in such a mood, feeling myself divided between myself corporeal and self aetherial. . . . Being freed of the weight of a soul, "capable of salvation or damnation", a grievous striving thing that after much straining was mercifully taken from me.'

Another poem declared a *Revolt Against the Crepuscular Spirit in Modern Poetry,*

> *I would shake off the lethargy of this our time*
> *and give*
> *For shadows—shapes of power*
> *For dreams—men.*
>
> . . . .
>
> *Yet God, if these thy sons are grown such thin ephemera,*
> *I bid thee grapple chaos and beget*
> *Some new titanic spawn to pile the hills and stir*
> *This earth again.*[55]

4

Church Walk, Kensington

'And then I found Kensington graveyard,'[1] said Pound in a broadcast of 1960. He may have been using the library in the High Street or taking a short cut towards Campden Hill when he discovered a narrow passage running along the west side of the Town Hall, past the morgue and then opening up into an area of uneven grass and battered grey tombstones. A little further on, round the corner, is the west door of St. Mary Abbots, rebuilt in 1872 by Sir Gilbert Scott on a site used for a church since the twelfth century. Designed as a companion piece to the Albert Memorial—with the highest spire in London—as one commentator said, 'It is a rather formal specimen of decorated work which conveys no hint of inspiration.'

The Walk itself continues northward, past a number of small shops, among them an umbrella and shoe repairer there for half a century, and a newsagent's, owned by the same family for several generations. To the left is a cul-de-sac of small houses, three-storied and narrow, built for artisans about 1840 before design had veered away from eighteenth-century simplicity. By the first decade most of them had passed into the hands of Jean Philippe, a character whose life deserves a book to itself. One of twenty-three children, he came from the province of Luxembourg with a twenty-franc gold piece in his pocket, and is said to have stopped a gentleman in Roehampton Lane to ask where employment could be obtained. Directed to a nearby home for nervous cases, he made a success of work undertaken there. Eventually he wrote a letter of proposal to the matron, an energetic lady of some means, thirteen years older than himself. After an initial refusal she came to think Providence had a hand in the matter and married him. After various ups and downs

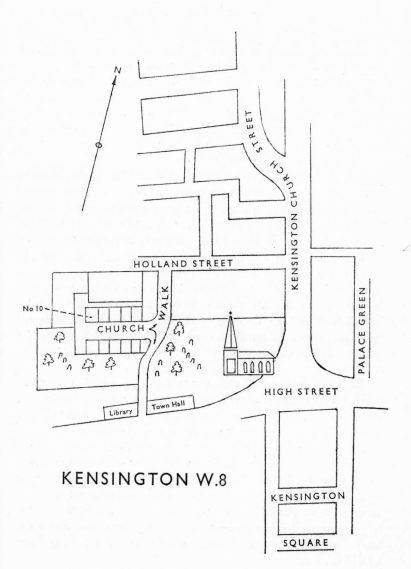

KENSINGTON W.8

Monsieur Philippe bought properties in Kensington, many of them of historic and literary interest, and it is due to his family that the Church Walk area has remained little changed.[2]

Ezra Pound, who probably never heard of Jean Philippe, was at once aware of the advantages of the position, in a quiet corner, near the Metropolitan Railway and various bus routes, his friends on Campden Hill or Holland Park Avenue. On making enquiries maybe he was told that Mrs. Langley at number ten sometimes had a room to let.

The doorway, hidden round the corner, facing the wooden fence to the graveyard and a few ancient trees, was not easy to find. When this was opened by a pleasant-faced woman, Pound found himself being led up the narrow stairs to see 'the front room'. With cast-iron fireplace, one hob on each side of the bars, and a pair of good windows looking south, this was the inexpensive and yet friendly background he needed. If F. S. Flint found it a dingy enough working-class house, Pound was later to write of 'my unique and treasured landlady'[3] who helped him and his friends, 'and she was a yeoman's darter from the farms to narth somewhere, I dunno wot nyme'.[4] When asked about meeting Henry James and other writers he replied:

'BUTTT [sic] in all this search for ggglory/ don't neglect the LANGLEYS/ positively the best England can produce at ANY level. Children must survive, and I can't imagine either Sam or his Missus as anything but vivi e vegeti.'[5]

The Kensington Directory gives the occupant of number ten as Henry James Langley and some of the neighbours knew him as Tom but for Pound 'he sure was Sam'. His father had helped to build the church and the house was shared with relatives. In another letter Pound wrote 'Any trace of the Langleys [would be] welcome. I don't suppose YOU keep two hens under the back [yard] whatever shelter. As to its ever having been LEGAL . . .'[6]

For a time Langley was manager of Barham and Marriage, a grocer's at the end of Church Street, next to the 'Civet Cat' public house '(as wuz) now degraded or at some time intervening era DEgraded to branch of Barclays Bank'[7] as Pound put it, and the curious wrought-iron sign is still there. The grocer's was moved across the road, near the church, complete

Elkin Mathews. 'I shall not forget that he was the first who accepted my work . . . and these beginnings count for more than the middle stops of the journey.'

Number Ten Church
Walk, Kensington, 1957

Woburn Buildings, now Woburn Walk, near Euston

with fittings—rich Victorian carving, deep brown shelves, names painted on glass, and a series of large Chinese tea-caddies.

Pound related how Sam 'annoyed his spouse by turning up his collar and collectin for some street signgers [sic], at door of respectable client of B and M who didn't recognise respected grocer (capable of imitating various local accents including that of "Reeefined floor-walker")'. Sam was fired when 'central management found curious homely methods/ such as cash cached in tea tin/ so that burglars wdn't find it if they tried the safe'.[8] Then, as often happens, Pound throws out a suggestion but refuses to enlarge upon it.

'AND other Chaucerian detail/ as when I emissaried.'[8]

As to Pound's bed-sittingroom, 'note furniture, inoffensive iron bed-stead. A very nice mahogany wash stand that folded down to look like a desk. Agnes [Bedford] may still have it, as I bought it and took it to H.P.C.' (a later address.) 'There were for a long time some beautiful Hunt post-Turner paintings, must have been three or more/ on loan from Violet. Think her Pa's name was William.* Fordie always complaining they had been spoilt by Ruskin howling for Hunt to FINISH 'em. Whereas Turner had the sense not to load on detail.'[9]

One of Pound's visitors noticed his table was usually littered with manuscripts, the fireplace full of scraps of paper. As Pound related, 'Gaudier's Embracers stood on the mantlepiece/ inoffensive table by the window. Books on top of low cupboard to the left.'[10] When Sam was shown the latest acquisition he remarked, 'Dew wot yu loike with me, think of a man cuttin' that in STONE.'[11]

When asked who used to come there Pound wrote, 'Actually IN the front room, Florence Farr reading Tagore, D. H. Lawrence missing train for Croydon,' and spending the night in 'sort of armchair convertible to cot'. Then again, 'Let's see, actually IN the room, Aldington, H.D., Brigit [Patmore], once or twice [Paul] Selver, Skip Cannell and Kitty on the ground floor [as temporary tenants perhaps], d'Orsey Hyde, J. G. Fletcher, of THAT lot of Paris Americans, Barzun, Flint . . . Fordie, and once W. L. George in court-yard/ you note window

---

* William Henry Hunt, water-colour painter, 1790–1864. As an afterthought Pound wrote. 'Don't think I much appreciated the Hunts at that time. . . . Now I should probably wonder if any école de Turner was as good, let alone better.'

is at convenient height for conversation from ground with inhabitant./[12] Don't remember Sloninsky actually INSIDE. Helston "Aphrodite" at Leatherhead.'*

Another item of furniture found its way into the recollections of Ralph Fletcher Seymour, a Chicago publisher, who called at number ten to find the door locked. This was finally opened by Mrs. Langley who had been mopping the stairs—a suggestion of oil cloth here—and she wiped her hands on a rag to let them in. When Seymour reached Pound's quarters he noticed 'books were everywhere; old leather trunks bulged with them, the limp wire-cloth couch-seat was held up by dusty tomes shoved underneath'. He also noticed a recent issue of *La Vie Parisienne*.[13]

Among those who came to the house during our own years there was Brigit Patmore, her hair still of that remarkable brightness which can never be imitated by the hairdresser, and the kind of eyes which Richard Aldington described as 'not aqueous not vitreous. You see reality in their shades of colour— the deeper parts of Lake Garda on a sunny day.'[14] Looking round the room she remembered humorously the squeaky chairs of cane. 'And it was neat and comfortable. Ezra made a home of the place, you know.'

There was only one snag. Pound, who must often have been up late with his poet friends, could not bear the persistent ringing of the bells of St. Mary Abbots. Mrs. Patmore recalled how he would cross the room with that peculiarly light step of his and shut the windows as soon as they began.

When Robert Frost called at number ten for the first time he was probably told: 'Go up: he's there,' for the household was not given to ceremony. Opening the door he found Pound in his bath. When reminded Pound wrote, 'Not improbable re Frost finding me in tub/ but not hip/ more likely byby's bawth.'[15] Supplied by cans of hot water from the kitchen boiler, —like an affair, as Pound noted in a poem, this very soon cooled off.[16] Fairly shallow, the bath was kept under the bed, being commandeered from time to time for a leaking roof or trouble with the plumbing. This can not have been very complex for the

* John Helston, author of *Aphrodite and Other Poems*, 1913. *The English Review*, March 1913, notes that he was a working mechanic, turner, fitter, etc. . . Sloninsky is mentioned by John Cournos as one of the Russian émigres in London at that time, the other writers are easily traced through their works but d'Orsey Hyde has so far eluded me.—P.H.

W.C. was probably out through the backyard past the hen coop.

Ford Madox Ford lived for some years in Sussex, not far from Rye, where he had seen a certain amount of Henry James. Now he spent most of the time in London and a formal separation from his wife seemed likely. 'In those days'—the early part of the century—'Campden Hill in the Royal Borough of Kensington was like a high class Greenwich village in which all the artists should be wealthy, refined, delicate and well-born. It was high in the air. In its almost country roads you met ladies, all of whom wore sable-coats—or at least sable stoles; and admirable children all bursting with health.'[17] When Pound was asked about his neighbours, many of whom were writers or intellectuals, he replied, 'District SWARming with 'em.'[18] Another correspondent remarked of his youth there. 'It was then full of errand boys and gentlemen's gentlemen, and servants existing in basements, but very good cooks.'

Once the region had been a mixture of farms and common land about a village to the west of medieval London and there was a time when Campden Hill Road, for instance, was called Plough Lane. Vines, grown in the district since the eleventh century, are now confined to gardens and courtyards, while at Aubrey House, home of the Alexander family,* some of the bracken once so prolific over waste ground, has been allowed to remain in a corner of the property.

What had been 'the Gravel Pits' became Notting Hill Gate, call 'Rotting Hill' by Pound and his friends. Isaac Newton is supposed to have died just above the turn of Church Street, and over at Holly Lodge, then reached through 'a winding lane', Lord Macaulay wrote the last of his *History of England*. The 'Old Court Suburb' centred round Kensington Square, contains the house in Young Street, where Thackeray wrote many of his novels and was visited by Charlotte Brontë. At number eighteen in the Square itself, part of the manuscript of Carlyle's *French Revolution*, lent to John Stuart Mill, was used by an unfortunate housemaid to light a fire.

Towards the other end of Kensington High Street, are the

---

* Among 'portraits of our time' Pound mentioned Whistler's *Harmony in Grey and Green* of Miss Cecily Alexander, in The National Gallery. See Canto LXXX, p. 546. He might have met her and her sisters at South Lodge.

high iron gates of Holland House* where literary and political figures had been entertained since the reign of James the First. Once Cromwell made the place his headquarters; at another period Joseph Addison lived and died there. Visitors included Robert Boyle, Horace Walpole, Wordsworth and Thomas Moore, Madame de Stael, and from America, Washington Irving, Fenimore Cooper. There are many other local associations of interest, some of them perhaps unknown to Pound at the time—Chateaubriand composing in Kensington Gardens, Talleyrand both before and after the French Revolution, then in the last century Walter Pater in Earl's Terrace, the memories of W. B. Yeats as a boy.

Ford not only told Pound stories about the Pre-Raphaelites and commented on contemporary London life but took him to see various places of interest. Thus in Canto LXXX:

> *where was the maison Alma-Tadema*
> *(with a fountain) or Leighton House†*
> *for that matter?*[19]

Lord Leighton, 1836–1912, first artist to be made a peer, in his Kensington home, just below Holland Park, made an Arab Hall lined with Persian tiles, roofed with glass mosaic, and containing old lattice work from Cairo. In the centre, always running with a cool fall of sound, is a little fountain.

'Occasionally with F.M.F. [Ford] for descint [sic] thru Ken/g Gdns' Pound wrote to me, adding the name of Gilbert Cannan, the successful novelist, who also lived in Kensington, 'During I suppose a year's tenure, along with Barrie's LARGE Dawg, et alia,'[20] When asked if this was the prelude to Cannan's going off with Mrs. Barrie, Pound replied, 'No, took 'em both.'[21]

If they met at Church Walk or in Holland Street, the three writers made their way to the narrow passage leading into 'Millionaires' Row', and also Palace Green, where along the avenue of full-grown London planes, stood the secluded mansions of the wealthy. With the royal stables to the right, they would pass the lamps with crowns on top and George III

---

* Destroyed during the blitz, the house has been reconstructed as a youth hostel, and the grounds have become a delightful park. Further details in *Kensington*, William Gaunt, 1958.   † Now a period museum.

on their standards and enter the gardens just below the Palace. Within the long frontage of red brick and high windows, designed by Christopher Wren, the rooms are full of memories recorded or forgotten—the winter night when Mary, sick of the pox, burnt her personal papers, William shutting himself away there after her death, or the young Victoria, hair down over her shoulders, moving through the corridors to receive archbishops and chancellor as Queen of England.

The Gardens were first opened in the early eighteenth century, when the court was out of London, to such people as could appear 'in full dress', then all the year round to 'respectfully dressed persons'. In Pound's time it was remarked that whereas in the reign of the two Georges, 'they were affected by the fashionable, they are now much more the resort of children and nursemaids'.[22] Then the leaf-sweepers and their smoking piles were part of the October mistiness, and until fairly recently sooty sheep used to graze across the wide stretches of grass and sturdy men with country accents accompanied by collies, could be very forthright when an undisciplined London pet went after their charges.

On another occasion Pound mentioned Cunninghame Graham's elegant figure on horseback, to be seen in the Row, as in Canto LXXIV:

> *Mr Graham himself unmistakably,*
> *on a horse, an ear and the beard's point showing.*[23]

On many days Pound must have gone out alone, and passing under the ancient elms of the Broad Walk, went towards the Round Pond, made for Queen Anne in the shape of a hand-mirror. The stretch of water seems to gather the variety of the district about its wind-tipped oval. In fine weather the kite-flyers, sometimes serious looking men and women, sit in a row while their swaying flags of colour rise high above the water, performing some projection of consciousness maybe, giving an imaginary power of flight. During a severe winter the Pond can freeze over and the whole landscape becomes a Victorian Christmas card, but on wet cold days in February the place is often empty but for a determined dog exercising his owner. Later on, in spring and summer, the sunken garden, with its waterlilies and arbour walk of lime, is full of flowers. Then in the hot, dry air of July, from the graceful little bandstand the red-backed figures of the players send *Cavalleria Rusticana* or selections from Gilbert and Sullivan across the deckchairs and strollers to the yachtsmen of all ages, who sail their chunks of wood or racing models across the Pond. In autumn all joys exist together when the water jumps up the sunlight and the sound along the granite edges is the continuous stipple of the sea against a boat.

As Pound wrote at the end of world war two, in the Pisan Cantos:

> *and the Serpentine will look just the same*
> *and the gulls be as neat on the pond*
> *and the sunken garden unchanged*
> *and God knows what else is left of our London,*
> *my London, your London.*[24]

5

---❄---

The Spirit of Romance

W HEN first living in London Pound had passed the Polytechnic in Regent Street and noticed that with the
expansion of adult education, a number of cultural
subjects were being introduced. Funds were getting low, and
according to Homer Pound in an interview given later,[1] Ezra
went into the Institute and when asked if he wished to enrol as a
student replied that he wanted to give a course himself. The
Principal was enterprising, and thus during the winter of 1909
on Thursday evenings at five o'clock Pound dealt with 'Development of Literature in Southern Europe' and the following year
with 'Mediaeval Literature'. Fortunately some details are available from the Institute's records. First came the definition of the
essential qualities of literature, dicta of the great writers—Plato,
Aristotle, Longinus, Dante, Coleridge, De Quincey, Pater and
Yeats. There followed a description of individual troubadours,
their poetry and the historical background. Via the Latin
Lyricists of the Renaissance the subject was taken as far as the
making of books and work of the early printers.

Homer Pound declared that Mrs. Shakespear and her
daughter were among the students. Wife of a London solicitor,
Olivia Shakespear had written a number of novels and was an old
friend of W. B. Yeats. They entertained a certain amount at
number twelve Brunswick Gardens, just above the bend of
Church Street, Kensington. The terrace of comfortable-looking
houses is still there, each with a little niche for a statue beside
the door, where the more frivolous caller might well have been
tempted to stand and pose. According to Miss Dorothy Shakespear, as she was then, her mother met Ezra at some tea-party
at which were American writers; also the Australian poet,

75

'Freddy Manning'* was there and Mrs. Shakespear asked Pound to call.² Therefore it was at Brunswick Gardens that she herself first encountered Ezra and being very quiet listened to his lively conversation. It is possible that the Shakespears were told about the lectures and agreed to go to the Polytechnic. Pound also gave readings in private houses and a lecture with other poets, at Kensington Town Hall, arranged by the Quest Society later.

Pound was working a good deal at the British Museum to complete *The Spirit of Romance*,³ 'an attempt to define somewhat the charm of the Pre-Renaissance Literature of Latin Europe', and 'to instruct painlessly'.³ 'Title was NOT polluted at that time/ wd/ be impossible to use now after three decades of STENCH,' Pound wrote from St. Elizabeth's. 'Think of an era when the word cd be used by any clean citizen whatsodam. Greater descint [sic] in 30 years than perhaps in any other 3 decades of history mentally speakin'.'⁴

The introduction rendered thanks to Dr. Shepard, whose sympathetic scholarship had first led Pound to some knowledge of French, Italian and Provençal, also to Padre Jose Maria de Elizondo for his kindness in Spain. 'Some stigma will doubtless attach to Mr Ernest Rhys, at whose instigation the present volume was undertaken. Guilty of collusion, he is in no way responsible for its faults.'⁵

The book, which first appeared in 1910, and has since been several times reprinted and revised, now contains a note, 'At least part of the subject matter then treated will not bear my present acids.'⁶ Yet the whole would show the detached critic Pound had started with a definite intention, and that which had appeared 'an aimless picking up of tit-bits' had been governed by a plan which had become clearer and more definite as he proceeded. 'The mode of statement, its idiom or jargon, will have to stand as partial confirmation of where I was in the year 1910.'⁶

Pound had attempted to present certain significant data on medieval poetry in southern Europe, of the Troubadours, of the Tuscans, of Villon, 'and, coming on to the Renaissance, of Lope de Vega, of Camoens, of certain poets who wrote in

---

* *Poems*, by Frederic Manning, 1910, contains '*Canzone* to Dorothy Shakespear'. Pound appreciated his *Scenes and Portraits*.

Latin—to make a sort of chemical spectrum of their art.'[7]

The 12th century had left two perfect works, the church of San Zeno in Verona, and the canzoni of Arnaut Daniel. Pound was interested in the intellectual mysticism of Richard of St. Victor and to him Romanesque was more admirable than the architecture of the Renaissance. 'Some temperamental sympathy may prejudice me in favour of this age.'[8]

As Pound noted further on, Horace wrote of his own futurity, ' " *Magna pars mei*, that in me which is greatest shall escape dissolution." The *accurate* artist seems to leave not only his greater self, but beside it, upon the films of his art, some living print of the circumvolving man, his taste, his temper and his foible,—of the things about which he felt it never worth his while to bother other people by speaking, the things he forgot for some major interest; of these, and of another class of things, things that his audience would have taken for granted; or thirdly of things about which he had for some reason or other, a reticence. We find these not so much in the words,—which anyone can read—but in the subtle joints of the craft, in the crannies perceptible only to the craftsman.'[9]

Pound was soon to meet that mixture of praise and blame which has so often been accorded to his work. *The English Review* critic thought that in this 'delightful book' there was a great deal of 'brilliant if a little disjointed criticism', yet Mr. Pound retained the stupid little affectations which marred much of his poetry. It was 'characteristic of his nationality' that there should be an incorrect classical rendering, etc., etc.[10]

In the meantime, Pound's work was appearing in America. Through Homer Pound's introduction, his son had at one time met Witter Bynner who later arranged for the publication of *Provença*, a selection of poems from his first two volumes. *Canzoni* dedicated to Olivia and Dorothy Shakespear, was published in London, July 1911 and according to Kenner 'contains many false starts, never re-printed'.[11]

F. S. Flint, reviewing the volume shortly afterwards, declared that if Pound could find a foreign title to a poem he would do so. 'Queer exotic hybridity! It would almost be true to say also, that if Mr. Pound can translate a poem, he will do so, rather than make one. He translates from Heine, Propertius, Dante, Pico della Mirandola, Joachim du Bellay, Leopardi; the bulk of the work in this book is not ostensibly translation but it reads as though it were.'[12]

Pound was in fact augmenting his earlier studies with renderings from Guido Cavalcanti and Arnaut Daniel, allowing them to impinge on his own poetry in *Canzoni*, 'a great fault in the eyes of those critics who think I should be more interested in the poetry I write myself than in "fine poetry as a whole." Personally, I think the *corpus poetarum* of more importance than any cell or phalange, and shall continue in sin.'[13]

In 1912 Stephen Swift and Co. published *The Sonnets and Ballate of Guido Cavalcanti*, which also appeared in America. According to Pound, the poet, born in 1250, was the greatest of Dante's precursors in Tuscany, the matrix against which the mind of the young Dante formed itself. He had chosen the *ballate* or popular song and raised it to the purposes of 'high poetry'. Apart from its beauty his work was interesting for his exact psychology, for an attempt to render the emotions precisely: 'emotions, uncommon perhaps, save in a land of sun, where the soul and the senses are joined in a union different, may be, from that which occurs in other countries'.[14] In his introduction to the volume of *Sonnets and Ballate*, Pound showed that there was in Cavalcanti no rhetoric, but always a true description, 'whether it be of pain itself, or of the apathy that comes when the emotions and possibilities of emotion are exhausted, or of that stranger state when the feeling of its intensity surpasses our powers of bearing, and we seem to stand outside and watch it surging across some thing or being with whom we are no longer identified.'[15]

Of course the Provençal poets had been studied by scholars and reconstructions made of their period but not in such a way as to give them contemporary significance, so that Pound's work gave rise to controversy. One reviewer found that Guido could be used as an interpreter of Ezra, who was effective where simple and direct but his graces and mannerisms were like a nervous tic. He had been to both the intellect and the emotions of Cavalcanti 'something worse than the proverbial traitor'.[16]

The Times Literary Supplement was more generous but pointed out that these translations must not be substituted for those of Rossetti. Those poems which had not hitherto been rendered into English, might not be fine poetry in Pound's versions but they were useful 'helps towards the study of the original' and gratitude should not be refused to anyone who had laboured to bring it nearer to them.[17]

In a letter written from 10 Church Walk, Kensington, Pound thanked the reviewer for his courtesy but thought he had been misunderstood. His endeavour was not to display skill in versification but to present the vivid personality of Cavalcanti, a man of very different temper from his associates. It had not been practical to reprint Rossetti's partial translations. There being one melodious translation with orderly rhymes there was little need of another. 'Guido cared more for sense than for music and I saw fit to emphasize this essential aspect of his work. The music is easily available for anyone who will learn Italian pronunciation. The meaning is more than once in doubt after long study. I thought I served my audience best by setting forth the meaning. Surely Rossetti's preface and mine should show the reader that there could be no possible clash between his aesthetic method and my scholastic one; he was as avowedly intent on making beautiful verses as I am on presenting an individual.'[18]

To return to Pound's introduction in which he declares 'I believe in an ultimate and absolute symbol or metaphor. The perception of the intellect is given in the word and that of the emotions in the cadence. It is only, then, in the perfect rhythm joined to the perfect word that the twofold vision can be recorded. I would liken Guido's cadence to nothing less powerful than line in Blake's drawing.

'In painting the colour is finite. . . . The line is unbounded, it marks the passage of a force, it continues beyond the frame.'[19]

It was the poet's business, Pound maintained, to see that the rhythm of any poetic line corresponds to a particular emotion. 'It is only when the emotions illume the perceptive powers that we see the reality. It is in the light born of this double current that we look upon the face of the mystery unveiled. I have lived with these sonnets and ballate daily, month in and month out, and have been drawn daily deeper into them and daily into the contemplation of things that are not of an hour.'[19]

Sometimes an ephemeral publication will provide a keyhole through which some limited impression of another living space can be obtained. *The New Magazine,* 1909, suggested another source of literary material but proved to be *The Illustrated Woman's Magazine* and indeed she was amply served there. A series of sepia photographs covered the contemporary theatre; Lily Elsie in the title role of *The Merry Widow,* Vesta Tilley, Marie Lohr and Dan Leno; in another show, a youthful and always dignified Marie Tempest, and Lillah McCarthy, wife' of Granville Barker, playing in Barrie's *What Every Woman Knows,* not to forget the comeliness of Gladys Cooper. . . . There was also a range of unnamed beauties, the pure maid, looking down at an armful of lilies, or the full-breasted lady with a fringe above inviting eyes. They suggest a masculine aim to own the first, so pure and spiritual, and if needs be find warmth and consolation beside the other. With increased education and the demand for political rights, a comparatively small but important number of women were in revolt against such attitudes. In England, Pound maintained, the Greek Pantheon represented the general types; Ceres the mother to anything that comes along, type recognized by the Eugenic Society; Juno, the British matron, with property and social position to be maintained, no one's comfort considered. 'Women of this type have always been, and thank God, always will be, deceived by their husbands.'[20]

'Aphrodite enough said. Pallas Athene, the much pitied intellectual. And Artemis. There has been a good deal of Artemis pose, and no one has taken much account of her in studying psychology. Yet among us, [in America] perhaps because we are a young and inexperienced people there remains a belief in this type—a type by no means simple—and likewise a belief in affection; in a sort of intimate sympathy which is not sexual.'[20]

'If we take sex lightly,' Pound wrote, 'it is because we think other things are of more importance.' Aware that every living writer was concerned with the subject, he observed 'that after the attempted revival of mysticism we may be in for a new donation, a sort of eugenic paganism.'[20]

By the end of the first decade, there was a growing concern with psychology. Professor Furnival, for instance, whom Pound often saw at the British Museum during the first years of his work there, had suggested the theme of incest running through *Hamlet.*[21] In America there was the work of William James.

Havelock Ellis had already written on the importance of dreams and soon the ideas of Sigmund Freud and others in Vienna were to become more widely known in England. Yet in 1914, as shown by a review of *Intermediate Sexual Types* by Dr. Hirschfeld of Berlin, 'the crass, ostrich-like stupidity of our national attitude on sex matters in general cannot be better exemplified than by the fact, which is not commonly known, that such a book as Dr. Havelock Ellis's *Psychology of Sex*, a work of international fame in the scientific world, does not even appear in the British Museum Catalogue'.[22]

In studying the poetry of Provence Pound could not be content with 'charm' and craftsmanship alone. However far back he pushed the search for the significant fragment, it was always to bring forward what was relevant to the age. In *The Spirit of Romance* he defined poetry as a kind of inspired mathematics, which gives us equations not for abstract figures, triangles and spheres, 'and the like, but equations for the human emotions'. Later on he was to see the poet as 'steam gauge, voltometer, a set of pipes for thermometric and barometric divination'.[23]

The central theme of the troubadours was that there was some proportion between the fire they held in the mind and the immediate thing ready for immediate consumption—a conception of the body as the perfect instrument which the increasing intelligence pervades, an idea which Pound had met earlier in Browning and which was to run throughout his own poetry.

Arnaut Daniel he found the best artist among the Provençal poets, trying new fashions of speech, bringing in new words, making new blendings so that 'he taught much to Dante Alighieri . . . and when Dante was older and had well thought the thing over he said simply "il miglior fabbro"—the best craftsman'.[24]

The work of such poets, he maintained, should not be judged by modern standards, they were not 'competing with de Maupassant's prose', being concerned with an art between literature and music, the fitting of words to sound—*motz et sons*. Later Provençal became weary, music and poetry parted company.

'The interpretative function,' Pound wrote in his essay on the troubadours, 'is the highest honour of the arts and because it is so we find that a sort of hyper-scientific precision is the touchstone, and an assay of the artist's power, of his honour, of his

authenticity. Constantly he must distinguish between the shades
and degrees of the ineffable.'[25] For the early troubadours,
chivalric love was an art, a religion, an aristocracy of the
emotion perhaps evolving from half memories of Hellenistic
mysteries, 'a cult for the purification of the soul by a refinement
and overlordship of the senses'. Some mystic had spoken of the
intellect standing in the same relation to the soul as do the
senses to the mind, and beyond a certain border, surely we
come to this place 'where the ecstasy is not a whirl or a madness of the senses but a glow arising from the exact nature of
the perception'. Similarly Spinoza said, 'the intellectual love of
a thing consists in the understanding of its perfections, . . . all
creatures whatsoever desire this love'. The art of the Provençal
poets was a preparation for *The Divine Comedy*, 'a single
elaborated metaphor of life, an accumulation of fine distinctions
arranged in orderly sequence'.[25]

In *The Spirit of Romance*, Pound maintained that at times man
becomes concerned with man and forgets 'the whole and the
flowing'. Hence the age of drama, then prose. There was sex
which had a double function, reproductive and educational.
'Did chivalric love take on mediumistic properties?' Were
there not certain times—a certain sort of moment more than
another, when man feels his immortality upon him?'[25]

Ezra Pound, working away in Kensington, continued to be
bothered by church bells. 'There is nothing more annoying
than to have chimes near one's home, chimes that are rung,
rung at all times and out of season. For they ring chimes at
weddings, and in Morocco they beat tom-toms at weddings to
drown out the screams of the bride who is usually nine or ten
and dislikes the ceremony, and with all this and motor lorries
belching out smoke in one's face as one rides [on top of a bus]
down Kensington Gore, I can't help wondering why we pay the
parson to keep up a lot of ludicrous institutions.'[26]

His protests to the Reverend R. E. Pennefather, who was not
wholly responsible for the noise, had no effect upon the members of St. Mary Abbots' Bellringers Guild, whose achievements are set out in dim gold letters upon black boards around
an odd shaped room high above the body of the church. The
ropes hang down through the ceiling and the mechanical clock

every now and then gives a jump and its wires ring out the quarters. A list of inscriptions on bells includes *Musica est mentis medicina*, and more ironically, when one has Pound in mind, 'The ringers' art our grateful notes prolong/ Apollo listens and approves our song.' The records show, for instance, that on Thursday, June 22nd, 1911, for the coronation of George V, 'a peal of Stedman Caters comprising five thousand changes' was rung in three hours and thirty-one minutes.

The ringing of bells became a symbol for all proselytising religions, the interference with the quiet of other people, an attempt to enforce the often sound propositions of the founders along with a lot of irrelevant absurdity. 'O Christian and bene-volent reader,' Pound says on another occasion, 'I am not attacking your religion. I am even willing to confess a very con-siderable respect for its founder, and for Confucius and for Mohamed, or any other individual who has striven to implant a germ of intelligence in the soil of the circumjacent stupidity.'[27] Later in the London period he was to write of Christ as 'a most profound philosophic genius, an intuitive, inexperienced man dying before middle age'.[28]

Even in 1938 Pound was remembering 'Campanolatry', or the art of bell-ringing, and provides a note,[29] 'in order that the serious reader (one in every 900) can calculate the personal dis-tortion in my writing. I was brought up in American school and Sunday school. Took the stuff for granted, and at one time with great seriousness. Questionings aroused by the truly filthy racket imposed on denizens of Kensington, W.8., by a particu-lar parson. It appeared to me impossible that any clean form of teaching cd. lead a man, or group, to cause that damnable and hideous noise and inflict it on helpless humanity in the vicinage. Followed this through Trollope and in the porcine physiognomy of other parsons. Vigorous anticlerical phase ensued.'

A story was circulated that Pound had written to the Rever-end R. E. Pennefather and that the letter was so curious that the gentleman had it framed, but like several other legends this was just too good to be true. Pound saw nothing on his desk when he went to tell him 'what a foul nuisance his bells were'.[30]

As a young man Pound explored religious ideas outside those of the various churches; for instance, some of his poetry reflects the theory of the recurrence of the soul. He became friendly

with G. R. S. Mead, who published *The Quest* for a society of
that name which drew together various theosophical and eso-
teric interests. Between 1890 and 1915 Frazer was to bring out
the volumes of his *Golden Bough* and their effect was considerable. When taking part in a controversy on the decline of faith
Pound reflects this widening of thought to bring together
mythology, ritual and anthropology. The following letter to
the editor of the *New Age* in 1911 summarises those elements
which were to be expanded and deepened over many years and
finally reach the Cantos.

'Sir,

'It is true that we no longer believe that the supreme and
controlling power of this universe is a bigoted old fool or a
Hebrew monopoly—this much the Rationalist has done for us.

'Our creed may run riot somewhat as follows:

'I Believe in the Divine, the ruler of heaven and earth and
in his most splendid protagonist, Jesus Christ, our Lord, born
of the Virgin Diana, succoured of Pallas Athene, Lord of Horus,
Lord of Rea, Prince of the House of Angels:

'but to say that we are faithless in an age without faith is
an absurdity.'[31]

It is unlikely that as a student Pound heard W. B. Yeats
lecture at the University of Pennsylvania. When asked he
made no direct reply but wrote from St. Elizabeth's as if he
became aware of the work later. 'W. B. Yeats in the U.S. in
1906 appeared to know more poetry than anyone.'[32]

On his arrival in London in 1908, Pound may have sent a
copy of *A Lume Spento* to Yeats or he might have waited until
Personae was out, but certainly by May 1909 he had been
praised by Yeats. During the previous autumn the Irish poet
was very busy with the Abbey Theatre; then came the illness
of John Synge and his death in March. It is possible that he was
in London during June, when the Abbey Players were at the
Court Theatre. By November Yeats had settled again in
London, his days 'full of all sorts of nothings', and the following month he wrote to Lady Gregory about music for a play
and at the same time mentioned 'this queer creature Ezra
Pound, who has really become a great authority on the troubadours' and had got closer to the right sort of music for poetry

than Florence Farr. 'It is more definitely music with strongly marked time and yet it is effective speech. However, he can't sing as he has no voice. It is like something on a very bad phonograph.'[33]

Pound described later how he used to see Ford in the afternoons and Yeats at his Monday evenings, 'Yeats being what Ford called a "gargoyle", a great poet but a "gargoyle", meaning a man with peculiar or gothic opinions about writing.'[34]

'Yeats appears to have been at once attracted by the intrepidity of Ezra Pound,' Joseph Hone noted.[35] At first he may have been rather formal with this ebullient young American, met chiefly in the company of others, but gradually that sense of new life and energy which Ezra Pound created transmitted itself. 'A rugged headstrong nature, he is always hurting people's feelings' Yeats wrote to William Rothenstein, 'but he has, I think, some genius and great good-will.'[36]

Rabindranath Tagore, when translating his poems from Bengali into English, wrote of having been given 'intimate instruction' by W. B. Yeats, in 'a quiet little room off the Euston Road'.[37] The Indian poet was probably first taken there by William Rothenstein and later may well have had difficulty in finding the house again. Many other visitors must have overshot the opening from Woburn Place and passing the massive ladies of the caryatids on the church—black now as the nearby railway station—they turned right again to find themselves in a neighbourhood little changed in a hundred years. The dairy with its china milk-maid and tradition of Dickens calling for a morning glass of milk, the newsagent's and other small shops have been there since Yeats first came to Woburn Buildings in 1896. Number eighteen of what is now Woburn Walk, is one of a series of plump, well-shaped houses with curved shop fronts below, linked by looped threads of ornamentation. Yet it is often the unremarkable that holds the half-conscious observation of those who live for years in a place, the curve and crack of paving stones, the way a door opens on to a hall and stairs go up to a narrow landing.

In a small room on the first floor, above the cobbler's, there were pre-Raphaelite pictures on the walls, a long box held manuscripts, and the bookshelves contained editions of Blake, Morris and Yeats' own work. Harriet Weaver remembered a later period when 'Ezra took some of us along after one of the dinners he used to organise. People asked Yeats about poetry and he held forth.'[38]

In Canto LXXXII Pound wrote:

> *even I can remember*
> *at* 18 *Woburn Buildings*
> *Said Mr. Tancred*
> *of the Jerusalem and Sicily Tancreds, to Yeats.*
> ' *If you would read us one of your own choice*
> *and*
>
> *perfect*
>
> *lyrics.'*[39]

The novelist, Dorothy Richardson, living for a time above the mason's opposite, also noticed the candles in the half light of summer evenings: 'and shadowy forms seated in high-backed antique chairs or standing clear in the window space; talking, talking, but in an inequality of communication, and, chiefly, being talked to by the tall pervading figure, visible now here, now there, always in speech'.[40]

William Carlos Williams has described an 'instructive week' spent with Pound during 1910.[41] First of all he visited friends in the country, much to Ezra's annoyance: 'Did you come to see me or the sheep in Hyde Park?' he exploded. Williams had enjoyed his glimpse of English family life, when little girls giggled at his unfamiliarity with boiled eggs in revolving stands on the breakfast table, and his host took him for walks across the fields. In Kensington one evening the friends turned round the corner of Church Street towards the short cut to the Walk. Pound in his 'heavy all-purpose fur-lined overcoat and broad-brimmed hat; as we passed a bunch of faded violets lying on the pavement he looked down. We both noticed the flowers. He stopped, hesitated a moment, then lifted them from their low position and—at a loss for a moment what to do with them —looked up and, noting the high, wrought-iron church-yard fence, placed the flowers on the bar connecting the pickets near the top—all with a swagger not to be overlooked.'[41]

At number ten Church Walk he shared Ezra's room where a candle burnt before the photograph of an unnamed girl and

Ezra made excellent Dutch coffee for breakfast. One evening with Mrs. Olivia Shakespear and her daughter, they went to Woburn Place where in a darkened room W. B. Yeats read by candle light to members of the Abbey Theatre. He had chosen Ernest Dowson's *Cynara* spoken 'in a beautiful voice, I must say, but it was not my dish.'

As they were leaving Yeats asked Pound to wait and he had a few words with him, perhaps mentioning a lecture he was giving on the work of the younger Irish poets. On that occasion Yeats spoke of how Lionel Johnson and others were consistently denied an audience in England. The chairman, Sir Edmund Gosse 'to everyone's consternation, at that point banged the palm of his right hand down on a "teacher's bell" on the table beside him. Yeats was taken aback, but after a moment's hesitation went on or tried to go on with what he was saying. Again Sir Edmund rudely whammed his bell—again Yeats tried to continue. But when it happened a third time, Gosse, red in the face and Yeats equally so, the poet was forced to sit down and the lecture came to an end.'[41]

One evening they went to hear a reading of Ibsen's *Ghosts* and on another occasion visited the National Gallery and perhaps the British Museum. Williams mentions the 'intense literary atmosphere, which though it was thrilling every minute of it, was fatiguing in the extreme. I don't know how Ezra stood it, it would have killed me in a month. It seemed completely foreign to anything I desired. I was glad to get away.'[41]

6

---❋---

Holland Park Avenue

While Ezra Pound explored Provence, Ford Madox Ford had been talking about starting a magazine; in fact it was already in preparation by the time Pound landed. Arthur Marwood, a country gentleman interested in mathematics, philosophy and economics, was one of the founders and some of Ford's wealthy relatives abroad may also have provided funds. The first number of *The English Review* appeared in December 1908, price two and sixpence for nearly three hundred pages, cheap even for those days.

'Our express aim in founding the periodical,' Ford wrote, 'was to print a poem by Mr. Hardy,'[1] *A Sunday Morning Tragedy*, a lament from a countrywoman whose daughter had died from an abortion, 'a poem other periodicals had found too—let us say—outspoken for them to print'. There were contributions from Henry James and Tolstoy, the first chapter of *Tono-Bungay* from H. G. Wells, reminiscences by Conrad, a piece by Hudson and various poems. 'You probably won't succeed,' Shaw wrote to Ford, 'but you will, at any rate, give your promoters a run for their money.'[2] Yet the editor felt they 'left the beach with the emotions of the oarsmen setting out for a long pull'.[3] Later he reflected that 'the record of events assimilated by the human mind today moulds the event of tomorrow, and the nearer the record comes to registering the truth, and so to render it as to make it assimilable by the human apprehension, the more near it comes to be a historic expression, the more it comes to being a historic event in itself'.[4] They hoped to discover whether there existed a 'sober, sincere, conscientious body of artists, which would try and crystallise modern life in its several aspects'. They wanted to put forth a quantity of good work sufficiently great 'to influence influential minds'.[4]

The second number included works by John Galsworthy and Norman Douglas: more space was given to poetry. 'We came upon the work of Mr. Yeats, of Mr. de la Mare, of Mr. Flint, of Mr. D. H. Lawrence, and upon suggestions of power in Mr. Pound's derivations from the Romance writers; and gradually it was forced upon us that there is a new quality, a new power of impressionism that is open to poetry and that it is not so much open to prose. It is a quality that attracted us years ago to the poems of Mr. Hardy and of George Meredith. (I know that my younger friends will start ominously at this announcement, that they will come round to my house and remonstrate seriously for many weary hours. But I must make the best of it.)'[5]

Ford's wife and his two daughters now lived outside London. He had taken two floors at 84 Holland Park Avenue, part of which were used as the *Review* offices, the rest as living quarters. Many writers, and hangers-on, passed through the passage, smelling of the poultry shop on the ground floor—no refrigeration in those days—and went upstairs, perhaps to find Ford in his quilted dressing-gown, opening the mail. At other times he would be formally dressed, just about to hurry out to some engagement. Douglas Goldring, engaged as a young sub-editor, was often asked to take a box at the Shepherd's Bush Empire down the road, and unless Little Tich or Vesta Victoria was on the stage, Ford would continue his work there in peace. Afterwards they were often up until the early hours checking proofs.[6]

Joseph Conrad occasionally stayed the night in the rooms above the office, with their pre-Raphaelite paintings and the desk used by Rossetti. About that time Violet Hunt, an attractive and vivacious woman in her mid-forties, became a frequent caller. She lived at South Lodge, Campden Hill Road, with her mother, widow of the painter, some of whose work was lent to Pound for his room at ten Church Walk. Mrs. Hunt had been admired by Rossetti, known Browning and many other Victorians, and written a number of successful novels. They entertained a good deal, bringing together writers and artists of different generations.

As a child Violet had gone for walks with John Ruskin, attended one of the first high schools for girls with the daughters of William Morris and Burne Jones, submitted her early poems to Christina Rossetti for criticism and remembered Oscar Wilde as a youth . . . 'in a big arm-chair tossing the long black lock from his forehead which America swept away'.[7] She was born, as shown by a lively use of English, with a sense of style, a natural selectiveness. Nowadays her novels—*The House of Many Mirrors*, *White Rose of Weary Leaf*, etc., are not often piled on a reader's desk at the British Museum but they are well worth a tasting. The period demanded a neatly tied plot and her strength was in delineation of the feminine imagination, in quick, decisive detail. There is an underlying concern with the break-up of marriage and the struggles of the 'new woman' to free herself, derived from Violet Hunt's association with the suffrage movement. Although surprisingly frank about other people's loves and lives, in her autobiography she is continually evasive. She had been sent to Paris to avoid the possibility 'of being dragged ever so slightly into a divorce case, a prime disaster for an unmarried girl in those Victorian days'. In his reconstruction of the history of *South Lodge*, Douglas Goldring mentions an attachment over a number of years to a married man, who died in Switzerland soon after *The English Review* appeared. As Violet Hunt and her good-looking niece went to balls and parties during the season of 1908 she was 'thinking at that time—all the time—of a freshly made grave at Clarens'.[7]

Violet Hunt declared that her 'years of mark and usefulness' coincided with the launching of *The English Review*. By a characteristic choice of epithet in her memoirs published in 1926, she calls the succeeding phase *The Flurried Years*. Although the book is centred round her relations with Ford, there is a generous admixture of facts and impressions derived from a youth spent among the Pre-Raphaelites and their friends. Like Virgilia in *Their Lives*, she had loved to walk 'Una-like, among groves of literary lions, with whom she ranked as a friend, an asset, a perfectly charming person of some literary value'.

Although Violet Hunt had known Ford Madox Ford as a boy and was aware that he had married and had a family, it was not until one evening about 1908, perhaps as Pound was installing himself in London, that they met again at John Galsworthy's house. Walking home together along the Kensington Road talking of the Pre-Raphaelites, they began, slowly at first, a friendship which was later to make them lovers. Soon H. G. Wells suggested she should send some stories to *The English Review* and she became a definite part of Ford's entourage.

Certain of Ford's friends became uneasy at the talk which ensued. Henry James remonstrated and Conrad declared, 'I cannot breathe in situations which are not clear'.[7]

There were frequent parties at number eighty-four Holland Park Avenue, where Hudson, Edward Thomas or Cunninghame Graham might be met; once Douglas Goldring noticed 'a little, quiet grey old man' who turned out to be Thomas Hardy. On another occasion Stephen Reynolds, author of *A Poor Man's House*, brought along a Sidmouth fisherman to discuss the possibilities of advocating better conditions. As Goldring pointed out, 'The new school of realists saw a chance of rolling happily on their backs, like donkeys, in their new found freedom'.[8]

One day another young man had gone up the stairs of 84 Holland Park Avenue, entered the *English Review* office and silently left a bundle of manuscript—but with no address, only the author's name, and without a word walked down to the street again. A few weeks later, when Percy Wyndham Lewis called there again it was a 'great and pleasurable surprise'[9] to find that Ford Madox Ford liked the stories and one was already set up for publication. Lewis's descriptions were usually acute, if not complimentary, and he found the editor 'a flabby lemon and pink giant, who hung his mouth open as though he were an animal at the Zoo inviting buns—especially when ladies were present. Over the gaping mouth damply depended the ragged ends of a pale lemon moustache.'[10]

'Born into a military aristocracy, life begins full of excited little bangs and falsetto war-cries.'[10] Wyndham Lewis's father came of a well-to-do American family, and, having fought during the Civil War, later he seems to have been without a career, leading the life of Transatlantic sportsman and dilettante. His wife was of Scotch-Irish descent and after a decade or so they separated.[11] At the age of eight their son had sewn his first books together, the pages decorated by 'stiff and hieratic friezes of heavily accoutred manikins', holding in bomb-like hands a hatchet or a musket. All Lewis's subsequent career was on the intellectual battlefield, a conflict with the pre-dispositions of his age.[12]

When at Rugby the other boys had been amazed to find him painting and his mother, herself artistic, managed in spite of their difficult circumstances to send him to the Slade. Later she enabled him to spend a good deal of time working on the con-tinent, mostly in Paris. A tall, smooth-boned and dark young man, he described himself at that period as looking like a Moujik, in clothes made by excellent tailors, with something of 'the tarnished polish of the English public school'.[13]

An entry in the London Post Office directory reads, 'VIENNA CAFÉ & RESTAURANT, (Nr B.M.), ladies dining saloon, billiards, smoking rooms, 24, 26 & 28 New Oxford Street.' Owned and staffed by Germans or Austrians, as Pound remem-bered, coffee was served with cream, real cream in those days. * It had become almost a club where officials and readers from the British Museum and some artists, used to meet. The first floor room was triangular, with a glass ceiling, reflecting all activities below like an inverted lake, so it seemed to Wyndham Lewis[13] sitting at one of the tables by the south window. He heard someone say that an American poet, whom one man described as 'crypto-semite'—an odd idea which still crops up occa-sionally—was to lunch there that day. He was surprised to meet a blond young man with fierce blue eyes and reddishly hirsute jaw 'thrust out with a thoroughly Aryan determination', whom he acknowledged with a certain mild surliness and soon ignored.[13] Perhaps Pound was growing one of his beards at the time; they tended to come and go.

Although Lewis thought it was Ford who had introduced them, Pound is emphatic that it was Laurence Binyon, then an Assistant Keeper in the British Museum,

> So it is to Mr. Binyon that I owe, initially,
> Mr Lewis, Mr P. Wyndham Lewis . . .[14]

The occasion was not a great success, for Pound's uneasiness,

* 'Also near the British Museum they served it smit Schlag in those days (pre 1914).' Canto LXXX, p. 540.

as often happened, was communicable and aware of the hostility of certain people there, who only thought in terms of Keats and Shelley, as Lewis noticed, he soon 'whirled off, bitterness in his heart, if I know Ezra.'[15]

When they next met Pound attempted to break into Lewis' reserve. In the Cantos there is a suggestion that Sturge Moore was also there, with his bull-dog as usual. When a certain point arose Pound said with narrowed eyes and mischievous goodwill, 'This young man could probably tell you!'. Wyndham Lewis soon realised that this 'theatrical fellow' as he seemed at first, was 'one of the best' and he began to enjoy the acquaintance enormously.[16]

There were men little known to the general public—Pound was describing London later—who 'contribute liberally to the "charm" or the "atmosphere"', such as Wilfred Scawen Blunt, the grandest of old men, 'the last of the great Victorians'. And Ernest Rhys, weary with much editing and hack work, to whom we owe gold digged in Wales, translations, and poems of his own, among them the fine one to Dragonet.'*[17] There was also Victor Plarr, one of the 'old' Rhymers' Club, a friend of Dowson and of Lionel Johnson.

Rhys, who came to the capital from Wales, had corresponded with Robert Browning as a young man and must often have told the story of how at a theatre he had seen the poet, looking like a prosperous banker or great physician, and while he hesitated Browning had slipped away. As editor of the *Everyman* and *Camelot* series, he was in touch with most of the writers of his own period or earlier. On his return one afternoon his wife, Grace Rhys, told him that Hudson, then nearly eighty, was waiting for him in the garden of their house in Hermitage Lane, Hampstead, which had a great oak before the door. After tea they walked down through that most beautiful and least known of London parks, Golder's Hill, through the little orchard where children pick up apples to eat, and down the avenue of chestnuts to where a pond is darker and greener among the trees. There Hudson noticed the waterfowl and remarked on the royal fern, *osmunda regalis*, which still grows along the edge of the bank on the opposite side, always strong and graceful in autumn, the colour of Burne Jones' hair. As

* Pound was anxious to have a copy of this poem but I could not trace it.—P.H.

Rhys puts it: 'A descendant of the fern Gerrard of the *Herbal*
saw in Shakespeare's day.'[18] *

In those days Hampstead was quite a long way from Kensington, and as Pound wrote: 'Ernest Rhys in Hampstead
reachable by motor bus—a few derelict hansom cabs in Hampstead . . . but top of bus means of exploring London from 1912
onwards.'[19] The older man describes these visits when 'Ezra
Pound . . . kept us in a state of comic dread lest he should
shock some innocent guest.'[20] One winter evening, when presumably the more starchy of their acquaintances were excluded,
Ford Madox Ford brought along a talented young schoolmaster
from somewhere in the Midlands, a contributor to *The English
Review*, and with his air of man-about-town, he introduced
the quiet and countrified visitor as Mr. Lawrence. During
dinner W. B. Yeats and Pound dominated the talk and at one
point during the Irish poet's monologue, Ezra Pound took a red
tulip from the central decorations and proceeded to eat it, stalk
and all.[21]

'I was next to Ezra,' said F. S. Flint, and 'I wondered
whether tulips were poisonous and that would have been the
end of him!'[21]†

Hugh Law, M.P., mentioned how Yeats had paraphrased
Ronsard and after he had spoken the poem most movingly in
French, W. B. Yeats gave them his own version. When
Florence Farr had accompanied her speaking of verse with the
psaltery, Ford Madox Ford contributed a burlesque sonnet.
Then, Rhys remembered, the young man who had been silent in
a corner rose nervously and very deliberately sat down at a
desk with his back to the audience and read in an expressive
but not very audible voice a number of love poems and several
in dialect. After half an hour the others became restive and at
last Ernest Rhys suggested he might need a little rest. With
an awkward bow D. H. Lawrence got up and retired.[23]

Apart from a few trips to Southwark, to visit John Cournos,
a Russian friend who had rooms there for a time, Pound declared that for months, possibly years, he was never east of

---

* John Gerrard, 1546–1612, in the *Herball or Generall Historie of Plants*,
specifically mentions the area.   † F. S. Flint suggested that Rhys combined
several occasions in his account. Pound's comment to P.H.—'apocryphal' and
'Ford—W.B.Y. NEVER at same dinner.'

Cursitor Street, just off Chancery Lane. Occasionally he walked over to Mayfair or into Paddington; only for a few months had he a visiting point in Chelsea. 'Problem even re/ Hampstead,' he wrote, 'whether one cd./ take time and busfare to maintain relations' with various people. 'Saw less of Rhys after approx. 1913.'[24]

Thus he came to know Kensington street by street and fifty years later was able to remember almost exactly where his many friends and acquaintances lived there.

During 1908 a fresh crisis had been forced upon Europe by the Austrian annexation of Bosnia and Herzegovina, contrary to the Treaty of Berlin. That August a leader in *The New Age* suggests the same bitter foresight on international failure which was to characterize the nineteen-thirties.

'Readers of Frazer's *Golden Bough* will remember the tragic figure of the priest of Nemi who sat and ruled by the grove and lake of Aricia until his murderous successor appeared. Even so is the situation of England in Europe. While therefore denouncing the false alarms raised by amateur diplomats intent on political capital, we do not disguise for ourselves the real nature of international rivalry. Thanks partly to the inspiration of Nietzsche, Germany is undoubtedly preparing to become the super-State of the world; and in the interests of civilization we cannot pretend to be altogether sorry that British Imperialism is being compelled to realise the price of power.

. . . The hysteria of the past few weeks is the product not of "jolly confidence" but a sense of social sickness of which increasing pauperism and unemployment are merely the symptoms. . . . If we had to make our choice, we would rather live under German rule than see our nation slowly starve under the rule of our English bureaucrats.'[25]

Although this scare was to peter out, the newspapers continued to show the increasing tension between Britain and Germany with regard to naval armament and the French anxiety to have military training extended.

The following year Ford wrote, 'We seem to see Britain drifting inevitably towards a war with Germany.' Later there would be another panic, 'and then some unfortunate incident and then indeed Armageddon'.[26]

The Annual Register for 1908 recorded that 'The economic outlook was becoming overcast. The high tide of prosperity had begun to ebb.' The year 1909 began 'amid political lassitude, with gloomy prospects alike in foreign politics and in finance.'[26] When King Edward and Queen Alexandra opened Parliament in February, they were cheered as usual, while a procession of wives and children of the unemployed, headed by women agitators, was kept at a safe distance from the Houses of Parliament. Bearing 'minatory banners', and accompanied by a car on which was a reproduction of a dilapidated cottage called *The Englishman's Home*, it marched down to the Horticultural Hall, Westminster, where delegations were sent to the House of Commons. Inside the House of Lords the scene was even more brilliant than usual. 'Two of the larger Cullinan diamonds were worn by the Queen.'[27]

During Pound's first year or so in London, the more militant wing of the suffrage movement was getting a good deal of sympathy, though in *The English Review* it was recorded that a day's attempt to sell *Votes for Women* outside Kensington High Street station—probably by Violet Hunt—had met with little success; people in the poorer districts were more responsive. Ladies had wandered down Bond Street in sandwich boards, others threw stones, and some of the Irishwomen potatoes, through ministerial windows. Yet at that time it was possible to declare that when Mrs. Pankhurst struck an Inspector, 'the blow was merely symbolic'—a point hardly appreciated by the police.[28]

Pound thought that the demand for the vote was foolish, it was a shadow, a useless thing. 'Ideas, however stupid, that people are willing to suffer for, always "win".' Those who opposed the suffrage laid up for themselves a period of future infamy. He wrote from outside the struggle but was as always, ready with a suggestion: there should be a woman's chamber, legislating on questions of woman's labour, etc., and its powers increased if it proved competent, thus doing away with the objection of giving suffrage to a lot of untrained voters. 'One would, of course, hate to abolish that picturesque relic the "Lords", though the thought of being even slightly controlled by a body containing bishops is both painful and ridiculous.'[29]

When reminded of these views many years afterwards,

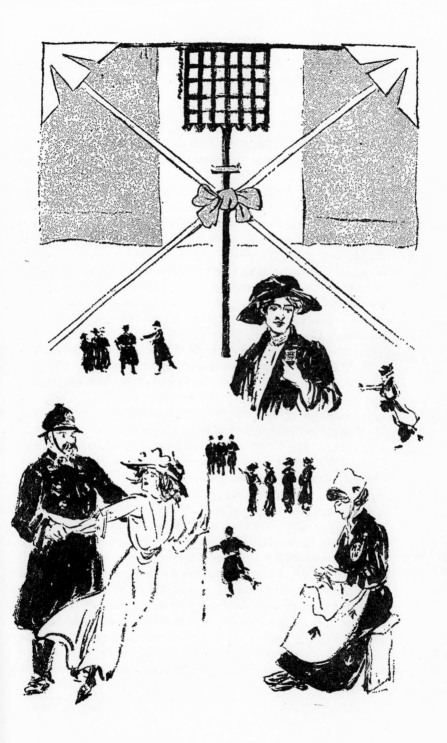

Pound wrote, 'E.P. had never heard of syndicalism at this time but same principle of people dealing with what they understand was there.'[30]

By the end of the first decade the struggle between the Commons and the House of Lords had come to a head with Lloyd George's audacious budget, which demanded contributions from the 'possessing classes' towards the increasing costs of armaments and social services, which were still very sketchy. The Irish question further complicated political issues. As Ford declared, 'Could anything be more depressing than the present state of public affairs? The two political parties have between them contrived to cause a class war of the most sordid kind, simply and solely for money! What could have been a purely domestic discussion as to who should bear the increased burden of insane competitive armaments has become a national struggle. The Conservatives knew that if they came into power they would produce almost exactly Mr. Lloyd George's budget but the lower Conservative party press, with all its evils, insisted "on introducing into the struggle the cat-call of socialism".'[31]

In May 1910 King Edward died, and according to *The New Age* all pronouncements of the real close of the Victorian period had been premature, 'spiritually King Edward VII had been the mere executor of Victoria'.[32] As Harold Nicolson has written, 'it must be remembered that King Edward, in the final phase, had been a perplexed and apprehensive man', and his son, George V, 'while still inexperienced and untried, was confronted with internal and external problems which, in their significance, intensity and scope, were incomparably more intricate and alarming than any which faced his predecessors'.[33]

There had been increasing numbers of railway and coal strikes and people feared 'the dangerous Continental theory of syndicalism, with its battle cry of "they who rule industrially will rule politically"'.[33] But as usual in England, ideas from abroad were to undergo considerable modification. Within the Fabian Society a number were beginning to doubt the Liberal-Labour alliance and the philosophy of Labourism itself and became interested in a form of syndicalism which could replace the owner-employer basis of society. At the same time certain minds were becoming increasingly concerned with economic trends.

'Even in the world of art and literature,' Harold Nicolson was expressing the official point of view, 'the old conventions were being questioned and new perplexing heresies being substituted. Mr. H. G. Wells and Mr. Bernard Shaw were already exercising a disturbing influence on the younger generation and forming many restless minds.'

Allen Upward found that 'in no other age since the birth of Christianity has there been so much curiosity about the future, the disposition to expect a new earth if not a new heaven'. There was much strife among those with good motives, and while socialism was 'the latest energy which is to transform society, at present it writhes and strains in the narrow sphere to which it is confined, like the Arabian jinn in the fisherman's jar'. Socialism, as represented in the correspondence columns of *The New Age*, was too much like a boiling kettle that keeps sending jets of scalding steam on to the hands engaged in replenishing the fire. It was power running to waste. Upward asks later, 'The promise of socialism was brotherhood: is its performance to be bureaucracy? . . . Is history to repeat itself further in the approach of another dark age? Such a question may sound surprising among all the din of research. But it is the quality of the human mind, and not its means and opportunities only, that makes the difference between intellect and stupidity. And it is already a truism that current literature and journalism are steadily declining their intellectual standard.'[34]

'What will the future make of the present?' asked C. F. G. Masterman in *The Condition of England*, 1909. The whole standard of life had been raised, 'not so much in comfort as in ostentation. And the result is something similar to that of the insane competition in armaments which takes place among the terrified nations of the world. . . . Where one house sufficed, now two are demanded; where a dinner of a certain quality, now a dinner of superior quality, where clothes or dresses or flowers, now more clothes, more dresses, more flowers . . . a society expending half its income in heaping up the material of disease, to which the other half of its income is being laboriously applied for remedy. . . . Companies rise like bubbles, expand, burst, carrying with them into the outer air their promoters and the parasites which follow in their train. . . . As to society, for the most part, it is talk, talk, talk; talk at luncheon and tea and dinner; talk at huge, undignified crowded receptions . . . talk at dances and at gatherings, far into the night . . . usually commonplace, sometimes clever, occasionally sincere.'[35]

Masterman, according to *The English Review*, had made a considerable contribution, particularly where he touched on the psychology of the poor, so little understood. 'Yet he wavers from hope to caution and ends by saying that he cannot tell where we stand.' The wise man was advised to go 'softly all his days; working always for greater economic equality on the one hand, for an understanding between estranged people on the other, appreciating always how slight an effort of stupidity or violence could strike a death blow to twentieth-century civilisation and elevate the forces of destruction triumphant over the ruins of a world.'[36]

Ezra Pound, who had found London so stimulating to explore, had come to realise for himself the realities which a few were trying to make clear. Masterman described the reaction following the fashion of high hopes, an indignation at the bankruptcy of things which promised much and accomplished so little. Civilisation, after its long jouney, spoke with less certainty, and it was impossible to see on the horizon the Golden City of men's dreams. Elsewhere he shows there was a conviction 'that the sparkle had gone from a society which suddenly feels itself growing old'.[37]

Ezra Pound gave expression to the same mood in his poem, first published in *The English Review*, June 1912.

THE RETURN

See, they return! Ah, see the tentative
Movements, and the slow feet,
The trouble in the pace and the uncertain
Wavering!
See, they return, one, and by one,
With fear, as half-awakened;
As if the snow should hesitate
And murmur in the wind,
and half-turn back;
These were the 'Wing'd-with-Awe',
Inviolable.

Holland Park Avenue

Gods of the wingèd shoe!
With them the silver hounds,
*   sniffing the trace of air!*

Haie! Haie!
*   These were the swift to harry;*
These were the keen-scented:
These were the souls of blood.

Slow on the leash,
*   pallid the leash-men!*[38] *

* 'I began this search for the real in a book called *Personae*, casting off as it were, complete masks of the self in each poem. I continued in a long series of translations, which were but more elaborate masks. Secondly, I made poems like 'The Return', which is an objective reality, and has a complicated sort of significance. . . .'

7

Cursitor Street

By the autumn of 1909 it had been clear that the *English Review* could not continue without further backing. 'In these islands,' Ford wrote, 'literature has never come into its own; perhaps never can.' In the minds of 'engineers, empire builders and moral or social reformers in this country, imaginative literature occupies no place at all.' The Frenchman registering himself as *homme de lettres* was welcomed by the hotel-keeper but here the political agent would say to the author, with a deprecating, polite smile, ' "Oh, please put yourself down *gentleman*".'[1]

Violet Hunt interested Sir Alfred Mond in the periodical but it soon became apparent that Ford was not to continue as editor. As Pound wrote, 'The EVENT of 1909–10 was Ford Madox (Hueffer) Ford's English Review, and no greater condemnation of the utter filth of the whole social system of the time can be dug up than the fact of that review's passing out of his hands.'[2]

Although Ford contributed his percipient editorials until February 1910, earlier he was saying farewell with a sense that his effort had gone unappreciated. It had been a splendid forlorn hope, an effort to make the Englishman adopt a critical attitude, it had printed some younger writers whose work showed a very 'high level of conscience. But it was obvious we could do no more than we have done. Our task has been rather, to discover whether there did or did not exist in England a school of literature at all or whether literature today was all and altogether a matter of disunited and disordered individual activities without tendencies as without traditions, without standards as without aspirations.' It had been shown that with such writers as Mr. Henry James, Mr. Conrad, Mr. Galsworthy and Mr. George Moore, the great mainstream of European international literature was cultivating still in England the muses upon a little thin oatmeal.[3]

It seemed to him that 'we produce not so many great lives as an infinite flicker of small vitalities'. Looking down at the traffic of Holland Park Avenue from the office window, he imagines the stage coaches of an earlier period upon the great western-going highway, 'galloping hard down the hill from the turnpike at the top, through the darkness against the black timber of the park opposite, four horses with lamplight on their shining limbs, their harness and their traces. There would have been the loom of the figures of the coachman and the outside passengers, very dimly to be made out; there would be the shapeless form of the luggage beneath the tarpaulin and there would have risen up thin and fine amidst the rattle of hoofs the sound of the guard's horn . . . there would have been these definite things to catch hold of or make a song about. But looking out upon the same highway today, one sees, as it were, innumerable motes of life in a settled stream, in an ever-increasing stream, in a stream that seems as if it would continue for ever. And for us we are glad we live today.'[4]

The naturalistic novel might do much to bring people together, Ford maintained, for although there were many more small contacts with fellow men, one had far less knowledge of how they really lived. If the arts had little place in the economy of the nation, it was because they still existed in the backwash of the Romantic movement, whereas their function was to be truly educational, concerned with the values of life.[4] Yet if things seemed rather dark to the writer, 'he must try to follow the canon of his art, and with sincerity and enthusiasm to express to the last word the truth as he sees it'.[4]

Although Pound continued to contribute poetry to *The English Review*, he had been looking round for another periodical where he could write. F. S. Flint had been reviewing verse for *The New Age* and he may have introduced Pound to the editor, A. R. Orage. In 1957 came a directive from St. Elizabeth's:

'Orage was the Pivot/ he and Ford outlast the rest of 'em.

Without A.R.O., Doug's Soc/ Credit*/ wd/never have been heard of. Don't play down Orage/ granite after a lot of the advertised. Wells, Shaw, Chesterton, all but the best of Bennett will have been sluiced out. Whether you can get into print/ as Cursitor St. not Kensington, and you cd./ be excused.

'The dinamismo of Cursitor St. Fordie floating in clouds by comparison . . . TWO kinds of Prose, impressionist, and controversial.

'Nacherly didn't mix.'[5]

Pound returned to the subject:

'Re/ New/ Age/ don't forget that Ford and Orage are the two men who keep getting LARGER as the time passes.'[6]

It was not only politically that the weekly was on the in-coming tide; the new movement in the arts and the tentative science of psychology and much speculative theory were to find a place there. G. K. Chesterton said that Orage 'very gener-ously allowed that monster, the Chester-Belloc, to roll and wrestle all over his paper, in warfare with two such giants as Bernard Shaw and H. G. Wells'.[7] Other contributors were to include Arnold Bennett, Walter Sickert, Ivor Brown, Wyndham Lewis, Katherine Mansfield, Richard Aldington, and St. John Ervine. Later on came Edith Sitwell, Herbert Read and many other important writers.

Orage, born in Yorkshire of a Non-Conformist family, was brought up by a widowed mother, his education being mainly due to the help of a local squire. He studied Plato and Nietzsche, read the *Bhagavad Gita*, and met Holbrook Jackson, who was later to write on the nineties and edit a number of periodicals. After a period of teaching in Leeds, where he became aware of labour and socialist ideas, Orage came to London, working as a journalist. Among his friends was Arthur J. Penty, author of *Restoration of the Guild System*.

Although he never belonged to one party, with Holbrook Jackson, Orage had been instrumental in starting the Fabian Arts Group, and later they acquired a small paper, which was initially backed by Shaw and a friend of Orage interested in theosophy. Soon there emerged 'an anthology' of prevalent trends in socialism, Orage encouraging both supporters and critics to express themselves in the correspondence columns.

* Reference to A. R. Orage, Major Douglas and Social Credit.

After more than a decade's work he wrote, 'The purpose of *The New Age* is not only to instruct and inspire and amuse its readers but it has a duty to its writers as well.'[8]

'Orage at Hulme-Kepplewhite parties in Frith Street,' Pound noted in a letter from St. Elizabeth's in 1956. 'Once at Lady Lowe's with orange tie.' The colour must have been unusual in those days for him to remember it.

Orage himself was 'a very engaging, though slightly feline person', observed Richard Curle, 'and this added to the originality of his views and his dialectical ingenuity made him a force with a large circle of young people; surrounded by admirers, he would expand his ideas with an airy nonchalance which half concealed his strong convictions.'[9] There was a tendency to be seized by enthusiasms which were apt to die away in time only to lead to new ones. There was indeed a grain of truth in de Maeztu's criticism: 'Orage knows the shape of everything and the weight of nothing but there was something noble about the perpetual search for the harmony of existence.'[9] Epstein admired his mental vigour and found a certain magnetism in Orage's make-up, an attraction of voice and manner, so that he seemed like a Greek philosopher with his disciples.[10] Mairet observed of the early phase, Orage 'needed uncertainty, the spur and tension of dangerous living; the life that engenders the courage of desperation. With nothing to retreat to, he was always facing the enemy. . . . *The New Age* was more than his, it was himself; henceforth he lived that it might go on, and fulfil its purpose.'[11]

Chesterton considered Orage, 'the most lucid exponent of economic philosophy of our time', whereas some called him 'the mystic of Fleet Street'. His views were centred round Guild Organisation and, as Mairet has pointed out, 'The new society of their vision was to be an organization made up of all the various groups of producers, each organized by itself upon its own principles of association. Certain regulative functions were to be exercised by the State, or by a special department of the State, notably the regulation of prices, but the financial proposals were not developed, for not one Socialist in a thousand then paid any informed attention to financial economics.'[11]

Whereas the political socialists wanted power, the collectivists wished for an ordered freedom for both group and

individual. Orage emphasized the middle way, the use of tact,
'to co-operate with the purposes of life, to enlist in that noble
service, the help of serious students of the new contemplative
and imaginative order.'[11]

Hilaire Belloc and G. K. Chesterton were then in reaction to
the progressivist point of view and their attacks were directed
against the party system. In 1912 Belloc's book *The Servile
State* emphasised that capitalism was unstable, collectivism un-
workable. In 1912 S. G. Hobson, a member of the Fabian
Society, published a series of articles in *The New Age*, demand-
ing an explicit break with the wage system and advocating an
entirely new basis for the worker as a partner in industry, a
possibility which was there in embryo in the trade unions. At
Oxford G. D. H. Cole was preparing his studies of *The World
of Labour*, published in 1913, and later was to make clear that
guild socialism should shape the policy of the whole labour
movement. As became evident, Orage had his reservations, and
while co-operating with such thinkers, worked to avoid the
sectarianism of the left, preferring to use the term *national*
guild. Then in 1915 the National Guilds League was formed
and three years later Orage's meeting with Major C. H.
Douglas initiated a new phase in which Ezra Pound was to
play his part.

Orage did not hesitate to attack the foibles of the moment or
the ugliness of misapplied wealth and never forgot the poverty
which the observant saw everywhere. Pound and his friends
came in for a few hard knocks from time to time, but in such a
way that it was almost impossible to be offended. 'I am fully
aware of *The New Age*'s limitations,' Pound wrote to his mother.
'Still the editor is a good fellow—his literary taste is unfortunate.'[12] When *The New English Weekly* came into being in
1932 Pound wrote, 'He did more to feed me than anyone else
in England, and I wish anybody who esteems my existence
would pay back whatever they feel is due to its stalvarrdt [sic]
sustainer.'[13] Elsewhere he mentions how during those early
years he did odd jobs at £1 a time, but those were the days
when tobacco was 5d. an oz. and a meal to be had for 1s. 3d.

Beatrice Hastings, who had attached herself both to Orage
and *The New Age*, wrote occasionally as 'Professedly Gorged
Saynsberrie'. When reviewing current poetry, most of it

W. B. Yeats speaking his verse in 1909

Percy Wyndham Lewis

'ambrosia rechauffée', she took off something of Pound. One book was by 'the modestest pote [sic] I know, and I have read —but then, everyone knows I have read everything. It's almost getting to be a habit . . . minor modern poets have no ideas, no diction, no metre.'[14] One of the poets mentioned by her was not long in pointing out that 'literary (nay, literal) abuse was not criticism'. In a reply Professedly Gorged Saynsberrie regretted that Mr. Kinross's verse 'should have happened along my week but I am not to blame. I am glad to see *The New Age* taking up its unique attitude in regard to literary criticism.'[14]

Pound was soon involved in a controversy on *Materialism and Crime*, maintaining that 'Practical remedies against crime are achieving results where preaching has failed.' The author of the original article 'appeared to deplore the fact that men may refuse to butcher each other on the battle-field in the name of patriotism and that other people would welcome such an advance of mankind. They would regard it as the triumph of Christianisation, which, too long mis-directed by the churches, has yet had so profound an influence that, even now, when men reject the religious form of the so-called Christian church with its bloody-minded bishops, they retain the teaching of the Christ, and practise more than was ever preached of His humanity.'[15]

Darrell Figgis, who had previously dealt with W. B. Yeats in a series on living poets, defended Pound's apparent strangeness, his break with tradition. He was at his best in the *Ballad of the Goodly Fere*. 'He feels, as many others feel, that the range of vocabulary in English poetry might advantageously be widened.'[16]

'*The New Age* of course the weekly going to press, took tea 2d/ and a cake or whatso/ 2d, in grimy ABC in Chancery Lane,' wrote Pound from St. Elizabeth's.[17] When the remark was mentioned to Arthur F. Thorn, another regular contributor, who later worked with Lord Lansbury on *The Herald*, he suggested we should go and see the offices in Cursitor Street which were blitzed in the second world war. Little now remained save the doorstep to a building which had once housed Bonner's printing works, and although we went up the staircase, only the walls were left and a few battered deed boxes.

One link with *The New Age* editorial office has, however

survived. If the A.B.C. teashop almost opposite has changed its
Edwardian dullness for chromium and plaster fittings, the same
wide stairs of carved wood lead down to the basement, where
those concerned with *The New Age* foregathered on Mondays.

Friends and admirers of Orage would arrive some time before
the staff joined them. In the far corner, waiting for Orage one
afternoon, Arthur Thorn* remembers a man in a cement-
coloured suit, with a stutter and a wisp of untidy hair across his
head—Arnold Bennett. Later others might drop in, such as
Katherine Mansfield, or Richard Aldington and Ivor Brown.

'One afternoon,' said Mr. Thorn, 'I entered Orage's very
small, dog-kennel of an office which was packed tight with
people talking. Leaning uncomfortably against a tall window
was a young man with a large hat cocked over one eye, introduced by the editor as Ezra Pound. It was like meeting a new
boy at the school. My outstanding first impression was of a
highly-strung, extremely mercurial personality, glimpsed in a
stream of sunlight that poured through the window. In some
way there was an uncommonly elegant look about the young
newcomer.'[18]

'Pound was rather restless, impatient and dynamic. We were
all talking about our contributions as Orage sat at his little
table, pipe in mouth, glancing around with a sardonic yet
friendly smile at everybody.'[18]

It was not long before Thorn discovered that Pound and
himself were exactly the same age, and one afternoon in 1912
the group at the A.B.C. broke up earlier than usual. 'It was a
wonderful summer day in July and Pound suggested that I
should come home with him. He used to cover great distances
in London and the two miles to Kensington was nothing to such
a good walker. He moved with such long strides that I found it
difficult to keep up the pace!'[18]

The two young men went up Chancery Lane and along High
Holborn, past the Holborn Empire where Orage and some of
his friends often went to see George Robey or Harry Lauder,
and then along Oxford Street, past the all-too-new outline that
Selfridge had built some years earlier and later as a bankrupt
watched from a window across the way. At Marble Arch they

---

* Arthur F. Thorn, 1885–1958. Actor, journalist and critic. Author of *Richard
Jefferies and Civilisation* and other studies. Bennett's phase was earlier, noted E.P.

turned down below the site of the old Tyburn gibbet, its associations annulled by the age of public lavatories. Along the avenue running parallel to the main road stood a few carriages under the heavy-leaved trees, the horses' tails tossing the flies away in the afternoon heat.

Where Kensington Gardens are railed off from Hyde Park, under the low-branched chestnuts, nursemaids or couples sit in the shade and the path dips down to the little valley and the Italian garden. Four great pans of water soften over the reflected sky, and only partly hidden by the trees, is the high background of houses along the Bayswater Road.

The walkers, one more conventionally dressed than the other, both good-looking, were probably too busy talking to notice how the ground again moves upward and the limes with their sticky sweetness leave a brown dust on the bleached grass, or to do more than glance at children and parents at the Round Pond. Crossing the Broad Walk, they would have ignored William III in his cumbersome clothes outside the Palace windows, and passing that group of ilex trees on the corner, found themselves under the London planes of 'Millionaire's row'. Then the narrow passage between the walls of a residence and the barracks took them out into Church Street, and they went by the café in Holland Street where Pound often used to lunch. Eventually they reached the small courtyard behind St. Mary Abbots.

'I remember Pound letting himself into number ten and leading the way up to the first floor room. There he flung off his jacket and set to work to make tea on the gas ring.'[18]

For a couple of hours they talked of books and people connected with *The New Age* or other publications. 'I remember Ezra gave me his visiting card and I must still have it somewhere. As I left that evening to go back to a settled home, I had the impression that Pound was a good bit on his own at that time.'[18]

8

Definitions

Unless a teacher swims with his times he will transmit the
ideas and attitudes of his own youth. The university,
which should provide a means of catching up, according
to Pound certainly made no attempt to do so. In America the
effects of trends in England thus lasted longer.

'As for the nineteenth century,' Pound wrote, 'with all
respect to its achievements, I think we shall look back upon it
as rather a blurry, messy sort of a period, a rather sentimental-
istic, mannerish sort of a period. . . . From the puritanical revolt
to Swinburne, poetry had been merely the vehicle . . . the ox-
cart and postchaise for transmitting thoughts poetic and otherwise.' Improvement had been chiefly in sound and refinements
of manner. Poetry as a 'pure art' revived with Swinburne.[1]

Rossetti, who died in 1882, carried poetry away from the
didactic, towards earlier periods and other languages. In his
lifetime Darwin had published *On the Origin of the Species*, 1859,
and Huxley's *Man's Place in Nature* followed in 1861. As if in
counter-emphasis 'Beauty' became the central word about
which almost two generations were to warm their well-kept
hands. The accumulating wealth from manufacture and empire
had made it possible for an influential minority to patronise the
arts, have splendidly bound books, richly decorative pictures
and embroideries and William Morris wallpapers. The Pre-
Raphaelite movement was in its way an industry, but in the end
the directors died and investors went elsewhere. Maybe the
aesthetic phase towards the end of the century was part of a
general uncertainty, an assertion of free-will, a pre-Sartre
existentialism in a society becoming more and more controlled

110

by business. Across in France the tendency towards clear lines, the unencumbered statement, was again emerging through certain artists, poets and expositors, yet by the end of the first decade they were still little known in England.

'Note, when I got to London the men who were old enough were all right; Colonel Jackson, Luke Ionides,* represented something hearty, pre-Victorian, they had something that Palmerston might have recognised as appertaining to men. It was Gosse's generation that was contemptible, mingy, they were carrots not animals. Born under the Victorian fugs, insularity, a meagreness, a dwindling.' Pound was looking back thirty years. 'The British mind in 1909 was decadent. I said so, and I got the languid reply, "but surely other empires have decayed. Why shouldn't we?"'[2]

At seventeen, Yeats remembered, he carried Whitman's poems in his pocket, yet was unaware of Hopkins, Hardy or Scawen Blunt, who were to opt out out of prevailing fashions. Over black coffee the young poets ignored the social and political changes in preparation and discussed how poetry could be purified and in Walter Pater's phrase, life lived as a 'pure gemlike flame'. According to Yeats, 'the revolt against Victorian literature meant to the young poet a revolt against irrelevant descriptions of nature, the scientific and moral discursiveness of *In Memoriam* . . . the political eloquence of Swinburne, the psychological curiosity of Browning and the poetical diction of everybody.'[3]

The Rhymers' Club brought together a number of poets who disliked rhetoric and 'scientific humanism' but with all this they 'had not found what ailed Victorian literature'.[3]

By 1908 Yeats had published what looked like being his major collection of poems and the Rhymers' Club no longer met. Much of the literary journalism of the next few years reflects a need for something different, further definitions, yet

---

* Pound used to meet Colonel Jackson sometimes when walking in The Rowe or at Leber's Restaurant in Holland Park Avenue. Over eighty, he spoke French well and was probably one of the 'old men with beautiful manners' of *I vecchi* in *Selected Poems*. See also Canto LXXX, p. 538.

Luke Alexander Ionides, 1837–1924, son of the collector and art patron Alexander Ionides, was a friend of Whistler, Burne Jones, Rossetti, William Morris and many others. His *Memories*, published Paris 1925, were written down by Mrs Shakespear.

there was still a reluctance to extend the fields of poetry, to take the townscape and the ordinary into consideration. Language waited upon subject matter. According to Ford in 1911, 'the old order, in fact is changing, the new has hardly visibly arrived'. As Yeats wrote, 'change has come suddenly, the despair of my friends of the 'Nineties part of its preparation. Nature, steel-bound or stone-built in the nineteenth century, became a flux where man drowned or swam; the moment had come for some poet to cry, "the flux is in my own mind".'[3]

Jean de Bosschère, writing about Pound and his poetry in 1917, acknowledged the help of the sculptor Gaudier Brzeska, in attempting to draw a portrait.[4] 'There has been an odd insistence in the way Pound has evoked the domination of the great writers. With the exception of those old writers who influenced him in his youth, he has treated other poets with a savage familiarity. I can believe that some of his inspirers might have found him disturbing, rather intemperate, often impertinent.'[4] Although Pound was to find the essay 'too high flown, too much about my noble soul and not sufficiently *documenté*',[5] he probably provided some details concerning his early development. According to de Bosschère, after reading Milton, 'At seventeen Pound admires Dante, for must one not first admire God and the Mystery? Before becoming united with the universal Mystery, one must worship it as an external thing. We cannot take a young man seriously who has not adored some formal God quite simply.'[6] Dante's clearness and strength of precision struck Pound's imagination from the first. Another poet was Thomas Lovell Beddoes, 'who greatly moved me at eighteen and for whom my admiration has diminished without disappearing',[7] Pound was to comment later. According to de Bosschère, Robert Browning, 'solid, unornamented, historical, first charmed him by his frank simplicity. I think one can say a kind of rusticity in the Camberwell poet attracted Pound's attention but not for long. He was always thinking about freeing himself from any indirect construction of phrase' and began to translate Cavalcanti.[8]

In an early poem Pound calls Browning 'ye old mesmerizer' and exclaims, 'what a sight you ha' got of our in'ards', while seeming to claim descent:

Definitions

Here's to you, Old Hippety-Hop o' the accents,
True to the Truth's sake and crafty dissector,
You grabbed at the gold sure: had no need to pack cents
Into your versicles.
                    Clear sight's elector.[9]

Pound declared that he began an examination of comparative European literature in or about 1901, 'with the definite intention of finding out what had been written, and how'.[10] He had read Swinburne and William Morris but seems to have avoided Whitman until 1909 as perhaps too strong an influence.* 'In America ten or twelve years ago,' Pound was casting back to 1903–4, 'one read Fiona Macleod and Dowson, and Symons. . . . One was drunk with "Celticism", and with Dowson's *Cynara*, and with one or two poems of Symons's *Wanderers* and, "I am the torch she saith".'

> *I am the flame of beauty*
> *And I burn that all may see*
> *Beauty.*[11]

The success of *Personae* in 1909 had encouraged Elkin Mathews to bring out a further volume by Pound that autumn. *Exultations*, of which only a few poems survived into later collections. Both the unacknowledged quotation on the flyleaf:

> *I am the eternal spirit and the things I*
> *make are but ephemera, yet I endure:*
> *Yea, and the little earth crumbles beneath*
> *Our feet and we endure.*[12]

and at least two poems suggest a concern with the writers' equipment. *Plotinus* refers to the vortex to become important to Pound later. *Histrion*, the word meaning jongleur, playboy or improvisor, defines the immersion in the best of a tradition, a process from which new energies emerge. As N. Christoph de Nagy points out in a study of the early poetry, the poet does not feel possessed by muse or anonymous spiritual force, rather in a very concrete way by the poets of the past. 'This is one of the two central and unique ideas in Pound's poetics which he owes to no one.'[13]

* Yale University Library contains the mss. of an essay by Pound on Walt Whitman in which he says 'His message is my message. We shall see that men hear it.'

Yet the absorbent psyche can only roll round the world in a pretty hard shell; to be misunderstood, even to be wrongly praised, is always an exposure of the nerve ends. As a young man Yeats had realized that 'style, personality—deliberately adopted and therefore a mask—is the only escape from the hot-faced bargainers and the money-changers'.[14]

'How many have I seen,' Pound exclaimed in 1913, 'how many have we all of us known, young, with promising poetic insides, who produce one book and die of it? For in our time, at least, the little public that does read new poetry is not to be bored by the same aspirant, and if a man's first book has not in it some signs of a serious struggle with the basis of the art he has small likelihood of meeting them in a second.'[15]

Exultations was not given a great deal of attention. After praising Flint's *The Net of the Stars*, the critic of *The Bookman*[16] found that 'Mr. Pound is a pundit. He has grown to be learned in many ancient things and then has turned to poetry again. Of course the poet in our youthful bosoms is not always a considerable poet, and if later on, he tries to sing, the failure of it may not always be because the time is out of joint. But there is a poet in Mr. Pound's bosom, and we would beg him to abandon his pursuit of knowledge and make us more ballads of the *Goodly Fere* before it is too late.'

Flint declared Pound the most alive of the younger poets and most rugged, the most harsh and the most wrong-headed . . . he used his language with such force, 'hammering as it were, word into word, that we can have no doubt as to his vitality and as to his determination to burst his way into Parnasuss'.[17]

By now Ford's personal affairs were in a mess. His wife refused to divorce him and he went to prison for a few days rather than pay a fine in connection with the proceedings. Then the idea occurred that if he took German nationality he could eventually free himself and marry Violet Hunt. When Pound was on the continent, probably in 1910 or 1911, he joined the pair who were staying at Giessen. In *The Desirable Alien*, 1913, both writers describe how with 'an eccentric American poet of tenderish years' they climbed up the Schiffenberg, on which stood an ancient convent and a ruined church. This was used to store farm implements and half open to the weather.

Definitions

There they found an old stage with two tiers on which miracle plays had been performed, its worm-eaten wood still retaining traces of bright colours. Their friend was 'a mediaeval poet, thin and hungry-looking, over six feet and an athlete'. Against their judgment he insisted on climbing one of the fluted pillars. 'Presently we saw him pottering about on top and declaiming his own verse in a sort of mediaeval chant which would not, perhaps, have disgraced one of the original performers. And then with an insidious crash, he disappeared and made his descent into hell, covered with the powder off heaven's floor, which he had gathered in his passing through the airy boards upholding it.'[18]

PLOTINUS

As one that would draw through
*   the node of things,*
Back sweeping to the vortex of the cone,
Cloistered about with memories alone
In chaos, while the waiting silence sings:
Obliviate of cycle's wanderings
*   I was an atom on creation's throne*
*   And knew all nothing my unconquered own.*
God! Should I be the hand upon the strings?

But I was lonely as a lonely child.
I cried amid the void and heard no cry,
And then for utter loneliness, made I
New thoughts as crescent images of me.
And with them was my essence
*   reconciled*
While fear went forth from
*   mine eternity.*

HISTRION

No man hath dared to write this thing as yet,
And yet I know, how that the souls of all men great
At times pass through us,
And we are melted into them, and are not

115

Definitions

Save reflections of their souls
Thus am I Dante for a space and am
One Francis Villon, ballad-lord and thief
Or am such holy ones I may not write,
Lest blasphemy be writ against my name:
This for an instant and the flame is gone.

'Tis as in midmost us there glows a sphere
Translucent, molten gold, that is the 'I'
And into this same form projects itself;
Christus, or John, or else the Florentine.
And as the clear space is not if a form's thereon,
So cease we from all being for the time,
And these, the Masters of the Soul, live on.

EZRA POUND,
Exultations, 1909

A poem in Ford's *High Germany*, 1911, suggests that it was on this visit that he thrashed out with Pound the question of contemporary subject matter allied to a straightforward style. The younger man seems to have defended the aesthetic ideal as far as poetry was concerned. In America he had already met criticism of the elaboration which was still fashionable on both sides of the Atlantic. William Carlos Williams remembered an occasion when his father 'had been holding forth in downright sentences' on his own 'idle nonsense'. Then he had become just as vehement about something Pound had written, asking what he meant by 'jewels' in a certain verse. 'Pound went on to explain with great determination and care' that these were the backs of books as they stood on a man's shelf. ' "But why in heaven's name don't you say so then?" ' was my father's crushing rejoinder.' Reminded of the incident Pound told Williams, 'Your old man was certainly dead right.'[19]

'The critical LIGHT during the years immediately pre-war in London shone not from Hulme but from Ford . . . in so far as it fell upon writing at all,' Pound wrote.[20] 'And he (Ford) felt the errors of contemporary style to the point of rolling (physically, and if you look at it as a mere superficial snob, redicu-

116

lously) on the floor of his temporary quarters in Giessen when my third volume displayed me trapped, fly-papered, gummed and strapped down in a jejeune provincial effort to learn, *mehercule*, the stilted language that then passed for "good english". . . . And that roll saved me at least two years, perhaps more. It sent me back to my proper office, toward using the living tongue. . . .' E.P. in *Nineteenth Century and After*, August 1939.

When reviewing Ford's *Collected Poems* in 1913,[21] Pound declared that Ford had preached 'Prose' ever since he could remember. 'He has cried with a high and solitary voice and with all the fervour of a new convert.' 'Prose' was his own importation. There was no one else with whom one could discuss it. One was thankful, 'in a land full of indigenous institutions like Gosse, and Saintsbury, and the *Daily Mail* professor at Cambridge'. The reluctance of Abraham 'to take these three upholders of obsolete British taste to his once commodious bosom, is a recurring irritation to nearly every young artist'.

Ford brought together some of his editorial and other comments in *The Critical Attitude* (1911) attacking the commercialisation of art and a growing disregard of permanent values. Ideas also put forward in *The Poet's Eye*, a series in *The New Freewoman*, September 1913, appeared with little change in the Introduction to his collected poems. His object was 'to register his own times in its own terms' and to urge others to have the same aim. The business of poetry was not sentimentalisation so much as the placing of certain realities in certain aspects. The gnat-dance of modern life was 'so extraordinary, so hazy, so tenuous, with, still, such concrete spots in it that I am forever on the look out for some poet who shall render it with all its values. I do not think there was ever, as the saying is, such a chance for a poet.'[22]

On a visit to Shepherd's Bush, perhaps during the Japanese Exhibition of 1910, he found himself in a great square of white buildings all outlined in lights. 'I think that what I hope for in heaven is an infinite clear radiance of pure light.'[22] The people were seen as a moving mass of black with white faces turned up to the light, moving slowly, quickly, or not moving at all. 'Pathos and poetry were to be found beneath those lights and in those sounds—the larking of the anaemic girls, in the shoulders of the women in evening dress, in the idealism of the pickpocket slanting through a shadow and imagining himself a hero whose end will be wealth and permanent apartments in the Savoy Hotel.'[22] Some would protest 'that poetry is written about love, about country lanes, about the singing of birds. I think it is not—not now-a-days. What we are in, that which is all around us, is the Crowd—the Crowd blindly looking for joy or for the most pathetic of all things, "the good time".'[22]

Although at first there might seem a contradiction in the statement that it is the duty of the poet to reflect his own day, Ford and his friends had 'rolled our humps mostly in a landscape that is picked out with the red patches of motor-bus sides'. What worried and exasperated them in the poems of Tennyson, William Morris and others was not their choice of subject but the imitative handling of matter and words, their derivative attitude. Reading was an experience that one should go through in order to find oneself. 'I would rather read a picture in verse of the emotions and environment of a Goodge Street Anarchist than recapture what songs the Syrens sang. That, after all, is what François Villon was doing for the life of his day and I would feel that our day was doing its duty by Posterity much more surely if it were doing something of the sort. . . . The main thing is the genuine love and the faithful rendering of the received impressions.'[22]

The actual language—the vernacular employed—was a secondary matter. 'I prefer personally the language of my own day, a language clear enough for certain matters, employing slang where slang is felicitous and vulgarity when it seems to me that vulgarity is the only weapon against dullness. Mr. Doughty, on the other hand—Mr. Doughty is a great poet— uses a barbarous idiom as if he were chucking pieces of shale at you from the top of a rock. Mr. Yeats makes literal translations from the Irish; Mr. Hardy does not appear to bother his head much about words; he drags them in as he likes. Mr. Pound as often as not, is so unacquainted with English idiom as to be merely unintelligible.'

Ford was trying to imagine the views and prejudices of the poet of his day and circumstances 'when he shall at least appear and voice the life of dust, toil, discouragement, excitement and enervation that I and many millions lead today'.[22]

Definitions

In December 1911 there appeared in *The New Age* a series of contributions, *I gather the Limbs of Osiris*, with an editorial note: 'under this heading Mr. Pound will contribute expositions and translations in illustration of the "New Method in Scholarship"'. Osiris, king of ancient Egypt, civilised and educated the people, his reward being murder. His wife Isis, recovered the remains and saw that divine honours were accorded Osiris as god of the dead. In using this title Pound suggests his own rescue work of neglected poets and the attitude of certain critics.

When writing to Professor Schelling in 1907 he mentioned his dislike of Roman studies but said he would endeavour to make his hate do as good work as his interest.[23] Throughout his life Pound seems to have continued to use adverse reactions, his own or those of other people as part of poetry or prose.

When reading Moore, Ford felt, 'a lasting hunger for the illuminating phrase'.[24] Conrad and James were poets in that they suggested more than was actually expressed. Pound wrote in 1911,[25] 'when I bring into play what my late pastors and masters would term, in classic sweetness, my "unmitigated gall" and by virtue of it venture to speak of a "New Method of Scholarship", I do not imagine that I am speaking of a method by me discovered. I mean merely, a method not of common practice, a method not yet clearly and consciously formulated, yet intermittently used by all good scholars since the beginning of scholarship, the Method of Luminous Detail, a method most vigorously hostile to the prevailing mode of today—that is, the method of multitudinous detail, and to the method of yesterday, the method of sentiment and generalisation'.[25]

Education should lead a man out into more varied, more intimate contact with others but a university training often created greater barriers. 'Any fact is, in a sense, "significant". Any fact may be "symptomatic" but certain facts give one a sudden insight into circumjacent conditions, into their causes, their effects, into sequence and law.' As an illustration Pound mentions a passage from Burckhardt.* ' "In this year the Venetians refused to make war upon the Milanese because they

* 'About this time, when the Florentines wished to form an alliance with Venice against Filippo Maria Visconti, they were for the moment refused, in the belief, resting on accurate commercial returns, that a war between buyer and seller was foolish.' *The Civilization of the Renaissance*, Jacob Burckhardt, Phaidon Press edn. 1944, p. 46.

held that any war between buyer and seller must prove profitable to neither." There we come upon a portent, the old order changes, one conception of war and of the state begins to decline. The Middle Ages imperceptibly gives ground to the Renaissance.' In the history of the 'development of civilization or of literature we come across such interpreting detail, a few dozen facts of this kind gives us intelligence of a period', 'a kind of intelligence not to be gathered from a great array of facts of the other sort. These facts are hard to find. They are swift and easy of transmission. They govern knowledge as the switchboard governs an electric circuit'.[25]

If only because our eyesight should be conserved we should read less—a reminder of the poem *The Eyes**—and look about more. 'The best of knowledge is "in the air", or if not the best, at least the leaven.' Pound has been trying to clear up 'a certain messy place in the history of literature' to make our sentiment of it more accurate, and thus the sentiment of the growth of literature as a whole. 'I am more interested in the Arts than in the histories of this and that, for the Arts work on life as history works on the development of civilization. The artist seeks out the luminous detail and presents it. He does not comment. His work remains the permanent basis of psychology and metaphysics.'[25]

Pound defines the 'symptomatic' writer, concerned with tendencies of the times, and the 'donative', who brings into art something not in that of his predecessors. 'If he also draw from the air about him, he draws latent forces, or things present but unnoticed, or things taken for granted but never examined.'[26] †

We advance by discriminations, for instance, Arnaut Daniel virtually re-discovered 'style', a manner of writing in which each word should bear some burden, make some special contribution to the effect of the whole.[26] There was a lot of muddled thinking concerning technique, some raging against it, others opposing free verse. 'Every man who does his job really well has a latent respect for every other man who does *his* own job

*   'Free us, for we perish
In this ever-flowing monotony
Of ugly print marks, black
Upon the white parchment.'
                  Selected Poems.

† Canto LXXXI, p. 557: 'To have gathered from the air a live tradition.'

really well; this is our lasting bond; whether it be a matter of
buying up all the little brass farthings in Cuba and selling them
at a quarter per cent advance, or of delivering steam engines to
King Menelik across three rivers and one hundred and four
ravines;* or of conducting some new crockety variety of em-
ployers' liability insurance† or of punching another man's
head.' The man who gets the thing done well always gets his
auditors' attention; if he be pleased afterwards to talk about it,
he gets his audience the moment he says something so intimate
that it proves him the expert; 'he does not, as a rule, sling
generalities; he gives the particular case for what it is worth;
the truth is the individual'.[27]

Exact expression did not strip poetry of its powers of suggestion. 'Our life is, in so far as it is worth living, made up
in great part of things indefinite, impalpable, and it is precisely
because the arts present us these things that we—humanity—
cannot get on without the arts. The picture that suggests
infinite poems, the line of verse that means a gallery of paintings, the modulation that suggests a score of metaphors and is
contained in none; it is these things that touch us nearly that
"matter".' Discussing the complexity of poetry Pound declares
that 'in so far as it is an art of pure sound, it is allied with
music, painting, sculpture; in so far as it is an art of arbitrary
symbols it is allied to prose. A word exists when two or three
people agree to mean the same thing by it.'[28]

Later Pound declares 'as far as the "living art" goes, I
should like to break up cliché, to disintegrate these magnetised
groups that stand between the reader of poetry and the drive
of it. . . . For it is not until poetry lives again "close to the
thing" that it will be a vital part of contemporary life. . . . And
the only way to escape from rhetoric and frilled paper decoration is through beauty—"beauty of the thing" certainly, but
besides that "beauty of the means," . . . a simplicity and directness of utterance which is different from daily speech . . .' more
dignified than that conferred by florid adjectives and elaborate
hyperbole, conveyed by the art of the verse structure, 'by

* Several themes here reappear in *The Cantos*: Alfred Fowler was an engineer
who undertook to deliver a consignment to King Meneleck of Ethiopia. The
Pounds used to go to his house, where Fowler probably related the incident.
Cf. Canto XVIII, p. 87.
 † This may have been the John Doe scheme, formulated by Arthur Marwood.

something that exalts the reader, making him feel he is in contact with something arranged more finely than the common place'.[29]

In the course of these definitions, only summarised here, Pound quoted, perhaps for the first time, the thinker who was to become so important to his work later. 'I detest that which has only a semblance without reality. As Confucius wrote, *I detest the cunning man lest he confuse equity. I detest the flowery mouth lest it confound truth.* I detest the so-called beautiful poetry lest it be taken for true poetry, lest it destroy in people's minds that divine reality which sometimes blazes forth, at other times is humble and modest, but always elated, always profound, and which reveals itself only at its own hour.'[30]

CANZONE A LA SONATA

(To E.P.)

What do you find to boast of in our age
To boast of now, my friendly sonneteer,
And not to blush for, later? By what line
Do you entrain from Mainz to Regions saner?
Count our achievements and uplift my heart;
Blazon our fineness, Optimist, I toil
Whilst you crow cocklike. But I cannot see

What's left behind us for a heritage
For our young children? What but nameless fear?
What creeds have we to teach, legends to twine
Saner than spun our dams? Or what's there saner
That we've devised to comfort those who part,
One for some years to walk the stone-clad soil,
One to his fathom-deep bed? What coin have we

For ransom when He grimly lays his siege
Whose dart is sharpened for our final hurt?
I think we do not think: we deem more fair
Earth with unthought on death: we deem his gainer
Who sets the world to fitful melody—

Definitions

To fitful minstrelsy that's summer's liege
When all the summer's sun-kissed fountains spurt
Kisses of bubbling sound about our hair,
I think we think that singing soul the gainer
Who disremembers that spent youth must fail,
That after autumn comes, few leaves remain
And all the well-heads freeze, and melody

O'er frozen waters grows too hoarse with age
To keep us from extremity of fear,
When aged poets pen another line
And aged maidens coif their locks in saner
And staider snoods; when the winter of the heart
Comes on and beds beneath the frozen soil
Gape open—where's your grinning melody?

High Germany, 1911.
FORD MADOX FORD.

9

---❋---

Frith Street

With his 'Method of Luminous Detail' Pound had not yet found the right term. This was to come 'out of the air' and had in fact been about for some time but as often happened during Pound's years in London, he gave a direction to ideas until then not clearly defined. The name Imagism, according to Pound long afterwards, 'was invented to launch H. D. and Aldington before either had enough stuff for a volume. Also to establish a critical demarcation long since knocked to hell.' Then he adds: 'T. E. Hulme was an original or pre-.'[1]

A little later he explained to a French critic that already about 1905 reforms of metric were taking place, before the French writers made themselves felt in England. He had launched the Imagists but the idea owed something to the symbolists via T. E. Hulme, Yeats, Symons, Mallarmé, etc. 'Comme le pain doit quelque chose au vanneur de blé.'[2]

During Pound's first years in London he saw a good deal of T. E. Hulme and his friends. Thus a directive was sent from St. Elizabeth's:

'HULME. Strictly Soho. NOT Kens. You can make Kens/ the centre of my activity, with forays into quite other atmospheres, Hulme's dinner circle and Fitzroy Street evenings/ quite different collections.'[3]

T. E. Hulme, who was to write on trends in philosophy, art and poetry, was another instance of a metropolis drawing fresh minds from its own hinterland or from abroad. Born in North Staffordshire in 1883, of prosperous yeoman stock, he won an Exhibition, read philosophy and for reasons which are

not quite clear—perhaps too violent an expression of opinion—
was sent down from Cambridge apparently with the largest
mock funeral ever seen in the town. After a period in Canada
roughing it, Hulme spent some time in Brussels studying
French and German, reading the continental philosophers and
giving English lessons. On his return to London, with the help
of a relative who made him a small allowance, he soon established himself as the centre of a small but important group of
artists, writers and intellectuals.

Pound found Hulme 'the outward image of a Yorkshire
farmer—the Pickwickian Englishman who starts a club'.[4]
Michael Roberts described him as 'a big fellow' with open
genial face, who walked with a rather heavy bouncing step,
leaning slightly forward.[5] With a large frame, and a certain
indolence which often goes with good health and a sense of
personal power, Hulme had traits which broke through into a
bullying roughness at times; an uninhibited emotional side
which resulted in action—he would take a person's arm in
emphasis of a point, or threaten to kick an opponent downstairs.
Wyndham Lewis, who maintained in *The Wild Body* that touch
was an important part of communication, must have found this
well illustrated when on one occasion Hulme held him upside
down against the railings of Soho Square.

Kate Lechmere, who had known Hulme in those days,
reached over to a corner shelf in her Chelsea sitting-room, and
found, beside an informal photograph of 'Tommy', as they
called him, the brass knuckle-duster he always carried. 'As a
sex symbol, not for aggressive purposes,' she explained. 'One
has to make that clear as quite a lot has been made of his
violence.'[6] As she also pointed out, Hulme made no attempt to
get rid of his original accent and Lewis, who may have had
his scraps and personal rivalries with Hulme but did not really
dislike him, described his 'nagging, nasal, North Country
voice'. This went on 'until he induced in his listener a sensation
of the cussedness of things which was really in its way a novel
cocktail. He was an excellent gossip.'[7]

Hulme was fresh complexioned, with curling hair: Epstein's
bust shows a rounded head on a very straight, erectly carried
neck and shoulders. Flint thought that he kept his ideas 'in
water-tight compartments',[8] but Hulme was young at the time

and perhaps over-emphatic. Forthright about his love affairs, which have since been exploited by commentators, Hulme believed in marriage and told Kate Lechmere that he would write no book until he was over forty. 'By that time I'll be a "heavy" philosopher'.[9]

Michael Roberts in his biography, while pointing out Hulme's importance as an assimilator of ideas, shows that he was not an original thinker. In attacking romanticism, pacifism, and the utopian conception of progress, Hulme was trying to make people understand that 'they were looking at things through one particular pair of glasses.' Neither a selfish reactionary nor a fire-eating militarist, he emphasised 'that the liberal romantic outlook coloured all philosophical thought in England and he claimed that this outlook was mistaken.'[10]

Hulme wrote verse, showing his work to a few friends, and about 1908 or 1909 gave a talk on modern poetry; as his notes were revised for two later occasions any shift in emphasis cannot now be traced. In 1914 he disapproved of the high-flown 'poetry akin to religion' attitude and wanted to speak of verse in 'a plain way, as I would of pigs; that is the only honest way'.[11] He saw poets could no longer be concerned with the heroic, big things, and quoted Chesterton's remark that whereas it had dealt with the Siege of Troy now poetry attempted to express the emotions of a boy fishing. Yet in 1908 Hulme cannot have been entirely unsympathetic to what we might now call 'the establishment' in writing. When Sir Edmund Gosse suggested that there should be a Poets' Club where poetry could be enjoyed socially, Hulme either became hon. secretary according to one biographer,[11] or treasurer in the words of Henry Simpson, the Club's founder and joint president with Henry Newbolt. At any rate, in 1908 Hulme circulated a list of rules which shows that the 'Poets' Club' met once a month at the United Arts Club, above Rumpelmayer's in St. James's Street, where dinner was 3s. 6d.; original compositions in verse and a paper would be read and discussed. Annual subscription 5s. Publication of members' work was also envisaged.

F. S. Flint in *The New Age* attacked such 'after dinner ratiocinations' and 'suave tea-parties in South Audley Street', contrasting these with the way Verlaine and other poets used to meet in obscure cafés, 'conning feverishly and excitedly the mysteries of their craft'—discussions which remade French poetry.[11] As to the Poets' Club, 'The Poets' Club is Death.' In replying Hulme called Flint a 'belated romantic' but nevertheless they soon became friends.[12]

During the late 'fifties in Earls Court it was possible to talk with Henry Simpson, a lively ninety-year-old, in a room full of carved dark furniture, many portraits and books gathered during that long lifetime. With red velvet jacket and a full silk tie, maybe acquired when the Yellow Book was on sale, he sits there beside a pink-shaded lamp and tea-tray, his mind shuttling back and forth between the 'nineties—Robert Ross draws him into the Devonshire Club to talk of Oscar Wilde's difficulties, or the period when G. K. Chesterton at the Poets' Club breaks a chair in the heat of a discussion with Shaw, or there is the young Ezra Pound reading his translations from the Troubadours. Also one comes close to the fear of those days that the younger generation would destroy all 'beauty' in poetry. Much of this opposition to change was sincere and contained regret for that un-urbanised life which for many town-dwellers had become a receding sunset glow of well-being. Then like some ghost of the future among those not yet forgotten diners, the interviewer listens as Mr. Simpson reads—recites rather— rhythmically, in full voice, one of his own poems, *The Long Lanes of England.*

Soon Hulme had fallen out with the organisers of the Poets' Club and Flint, ignoring the prior organisation, later described how, 'Somewhere in the gloom of 1908 Mr. T. E. Hulme . . . excited by the propinquity, at a half-a-crown dance, of the other sex (if, as Remy de Gourmont avers, the passage from the aesthetic to the sexual emotion *n'est qu'un pas*, the reverse is surely also true) proposed to a companion that they should form a poets' club. Thus a number of poets began to dine together.'[13] There was no formal organisation. Edward Storer had already published *Inclinations* and followed with *Mirrors of Illusion.* which included an essay attacking current conventions in poetry.

Hulme, together with F. W. Tancred, was said to have spent hours each day searching for the right phrase, 'absolutely accurate presentation and no verbiage'.[13] There was also a good deal about French poetry, which Flint was studying in detail. On April 22nd 1909, Ezra Pound, whose *Personae* had been published the previous Friday, was introduced to them by Florence Farr and Desmond FitzGerald. At that stage Flint declared, 'he could not be made to believe there was any French poetry after Ronsard. He was full of his troubadours but I do not remember that he did more than attempt to illustrate (or refute) our theories occasionally with their example.'[13] Pound found little agreement between the poets: Hulme seemed to be trying to convince people of something without much success and there was little or no formulation.[14] Hulme was the largest object in his dining club, Pound wrote later, his satellites in 1909 being Storer, Flint, and the 'dark man from the north' who wrote 'The Gilly of Christ' and later took to printing his name in Gaelic [Joseph Campbell]. Desmond FitzGerald was in fairly regular attendance but not to be called a satellite.[15]

From St. Elizabeth's he considered: 'Hulme's gang: Tancred (Hulme said he created him) a perfect museum piece; Storer, Flint, enslaved to translate stuff T.E.H. got options on, [probably Bergson's work] I forget whether it was F/ or Storer who thought Hulme "dangerous"; FitzGerald, Colum [there] once or twice, [Ashley] Dukes showed up at Frith Street in evening but don't remember him at Tour Eiffel.'*[16]

In 1911 Hulme met and became friendly with Mrs. Ethel Kepplewhite who lived with her father at 67 Frith Street, a fine Georgian house said to have been the Venetian Embassy. Although he had rooms elsewhere Hulme worked and entertained there. Mrs. Kepplewhite, separated from her husband, in the words of Ashley Dukes, 'was a woman capable of great devotion to her friends'.[17] J. C. Squire described how large numbers of people, writers, painters, philosophers and patrons met at Frith Street and Hulme, 'massive as Johnson but a nonsmoker and a tee-totaller, consumed sweets, argued with everybody who was able to cope with him' . . . sometimes he talked great nonsense and he was fully aware of the fact but not all his listeners were. 'Always his talk was fluent, well-shaped, subtle, he was combative, fiery-tempered, intolerant of those who crossed him, catholic otherwise in his tastes and his friends, an utter individualist in his habits, and afraid of nobody. . . .

* Soho restaurant.

Though his views fluctuated there was always behind his thought an endeavour to relate things.'[18]

Pound noted, 'Epstein at Frith Street. Hulme boosting the Flenites.* I doubt if anyone else would have at that time.'[19]

Jacob Epstein also described those Thursday evenings in his memoirs. When the book was mentioned to Pound he replied, imitating Epstein, 'Whoz "autobiography", YAKOB'S who tuk iz pen in 'and? Effect of Hulme's providing him with a vocabulary was a JOYE in that era.'[20]

Thus through Hulme and his friends Pound was in touch with a great many more people in London. There was a weekly show of painters and sculptors at the Camden Group in Fitzroy Street and later near the Cumberland market. Afterwards exhibitors and their friends dined at the Old Sceptre Chop House, Goslings, off Regent Street or at the Tour Eiffel in Percy Street. There on one occasion Pound declaimed his *Sestina Altaforte* with such vigour that the management placed a screen round their table, and a few astonished diners looked over to see what was going on at the other side. Sometimes they met at the Café Royal, where Hulme would be teased about his liking for suet pudding and treacle. Indeed there was no need of stimulants to make him comical or entertaining.

Epstein shows that some people thought him arrogant and a bully but in reality he had a candid and original nature. 'His intolerance of sham made him feared.' Yet, Epstein goes on, in many ways he was lazy and in no hurry; a good talker, he thought he had plenty of time in which to do his work, marry and have a family.[21]

* A series of carvings by Epstein.

10

Holland Street

Pound's concern with 'the ancients', his talk with Ford, Hulme and other writers, was part of a general uneasiness, a pause before a new means of expression could be found. How was poetry to move among contemporary men and women and keep its difference but not distance?

At that time a new grouping was taking place, round Harold Monro, who edited *Poetry Review*, later to become *Poetry and Drama*. This brought together the rather more traditional poets and some of those whom Ford called 'les jeunes'. Aided by his handsome and intelligent wife, Monro opened the Poetry Bookshop in Devonshire Street, and lectures and discussions were arranged there. Alida Monro remembered travelling one day by underground to Golders Green in the same carriage as a remarkable young man in a velvet suit. 'You couldn't help noticing him.'[1] Outside the station he entered the Lady Bachelor Chambers and she realised later he was probably visiting H.D. and other compatriots then in London. When told of this memory, Pound replied, 'Coat, not suit. Grey velvet.'[2]

A good deal has been made of Pound's choice of clothes at this time, when there was little between the formal and the 'arty'. 'We often wondered who on earth was his tailor,' one acquaintance said. When told the remark, Pound was amused and wrote from St. Elizabeth's Hospital:

'Cotton of Holland Street during LONG period. Poole for high swank in prosperity when briefly attained. I don't imagine HE wants it mentioned. Peak of attainment annoyed elderly brit/ literatus.'

'There were UNIQUE moments on the heights.'[3]

Mr. Wilkinson (the novelist Louis Marlow) spoke of that

period in a broadcast long afterwards. 'Ezra Pound was a very young man I remember when I knew him first in 1912, and how very striking he was, his personality, his dress even; he dressed congruously with himself, very unusually you see, very remarkably and very full of colour. You couldn't help noticing his dress as it matched him exactly. He was a very good looking young man. . . .'*

This is a diversion from the theme of literary affairs in 1911–12 when a controversy had arisen in *The Spectator* between those who believed in strict scansion and the advocates of free verse. Then Pound published a *credo*, in *Poetry Review* for February, 1912, declaring that he would prefer to play tennis rather than discuss any theories or processes of art. The poets would meet in a Soho restaurant, at another time in some drawing-room over tea and thus one survived the resignation of Mr. Balfour, the iniquities of the American customs, and what was worse, the periodic press. 'And then in the middle of it, there being apparently no other person at once capable and available one is stopped and asked to explain oneself.'⁴

He believed in an 'absolute rhythm', poetry which corresponds exactly to the emotion or shade of emotion to be expressed. The proper and perfect symbol was the natural object and if used its symbolic function must not intrude. Technique was the test of a writer's sincerity. As to form there was a 'fluid' as well as a 'solid' content; some poems may have form as a tree has form, some as water poured into a vase. The artist must master all known forms and systems of metric. 'I have with some persistence set about this, searching particularly into those periods wherein the systems came to birth or attained their maturity. It has been complained, with some justice, that I dump my notebooks on the public.' Only after a long struggle could poetry attain such a degree of development, or modernity, as to vitally concern people who were accustomed in prose to such writers as Henry James and Anatole France,† or in music to Debussy. As Chaucer had written, 'The lyf so short, the craft so long to lerne.'⁴

Then Pound declared, 'My pawing over the ancients and

---

* In the Third Programme, February 1st, 1964.
† See *Literary Essays*, pp. 9–11, for the argument in detail. At that point the novel had indeed 'picked up' the growing interest in psychology before poetry.

semi-ancients has been one struggle to find out what has been done, once for all, better than it can ever be done again, and to find out what remains for us to do, and plenty does remain, for if we still feel the same emotions as those which launched the thousand ships, it is quite certain that we come on these feelings differently, through different nuances, by different intellectual gradations. Each age has its own abounding gifts, yet only some ages transmute them into matter of duration. No good poetry is written in a manner which is twenty years old, for to write in such a manner shows conclusively that the writer thinks from books, convention and *cliché*, and not from life, yet a man feeling the divorce of life and his art may naturally try to resurrect a forgotten mode if he finds in that mode some leaven, or if he thinks he sees in it some element lacking in contemporary art which might unite that art again to its sustenance, life.'[4]

W. B. Yeats, who had become a classic in his own life-time, had stripped English poetry of its rhetoric and done away with inversions. Robert Bridges, Maurice Hewlett and Frederic Manning were, in their different ways, seriously concerned with overhauling the metric, in testing the language and its adaptability to certain modes. Ford was making experiments in modernity.[4]

'As to twentieth century poetry,' Pound concluded his article of 1912, 'and the poetry which I expect to see written during the next decade or so, it will, I think, move against poppy-cock, it will be harder and saner, it will be what Mr. Hewlett calls "nearer the bone". It will be as much like granite as it can be, its force will lie in its truth, its interpretative power (of course poetic force does always rest there): I mean it will not try to seem forcible by rhetorical din, and luxurious riot. We will have fewer painted adjectives impeding the shock and stroke of it. At least for myself, I want it so, austere, direct, free from emotional slither.'[4]

Henry Newbolt in *A New Study of English Poetry* mentioned a critic who was also a poet whom he read with interest (i.e. Pound) who had described his struggle to find out what should be done, etc. Of course there could be no real duplication. An even more distinguished writer had lately made emphatic use of the word 'pattern' in his description of poetry. 'I do not attribute any heretical intention to either of these writers,'

Newbolt continued, 'but it is within my knowledge that they
have been quoted to support the theory of an external standard,
of types of beauty to which poems should conform.' If every
work of art were simply the expression of the artist's intuition,
it is evident that a pattern would be useless, since it would
be expressed by different minds. Yet he found the effort for
freedom being made with unexampled vigour and intelligence.
'We are witnessing the natural recovery from a period of
decadence. What poet has to learn from poet is not a trick of
the hand or a set of cadences nor a formula or an orthodox
tradition but a passion for sincerity. . . . Poets are bent on
getting nearer to the inward melody, on moving more faithfully
to the inward rhythm.' This was not lawlessness, nor a cult of
the ugly or eccentric. 'I see and I desire others to see in it the
old and true instinct of English poets, the belief that formal
beauty is begotten not of the hand of the artist but of the
spirit.'

When dealing with poetry and personality, Newbolt quotes
Sidney's 'Sonnets of Astrophel', *Fool, said my Muse to me, look
in thy heart and write.* His conclusion now seems Jungian, 'It
may be there is in poetry a power to reach a still deeper truth, a
still profounder being, to draw at times directly from that un-
seen, unsounded Pool of Personality of which our lives are but
momentary jets flung into the sunlight.'[5]

'My generation,' as Pound summarised it, 'found criticism
of the arts cluttered with the work of men who persistently
defined the work of one art in terms of another. For a decade or
two we tried to get the arts sorted out. . . . For a few years
painters and sculptors tried to limit themselves to colour and
form. And this did, I believe, clarify the minds of a small group
of serious people. We traced the "just word" back to Flaubert,
we heard a good deal about using it. For the purpose of novel
writing and the telling of stories, the composition of poems, the
evocative word, the word that throws a vivid image on the
mind of the reader suffices.'[6]

It has been said that Pound snaffled the ideas for the movement which became Imagism from T. E. Hulme, who as far as
the present writer is aware, never said this himself. 'He was too
concerned with his own work,' Kate Lechmere commented,
'thinking things out and trying to build up a relationship of

ideas to be used later.'⁷ Later on Pound remarked, 'It is a matter of infinitesimal importance but still. . . . The name first appears in my introduction to T. E. Hulme at the end of *Ripostes*, and the whole affair was started, not very seriously, chiefly to get H.D.'s five poems a hearing. It began certainly in Church Walk with H.D., Richard and myself. . . . But I don't suppose it matters a t'uppeny damn!'⁸

Poetry and Drama for June 1913 mentioned 'a new school of English poetry, still at present very small and under the formidable dictatorship of Ezra Pound'. According to Richard Aldington, a young writer lately come from home and school in Dover, this began in 'the infernal bunshop' full of English spinsters. 'The Imagist mouve*mong* was born in a teashop—in the Royal Borough of Kensington.'⁹

On the opposite side of Church Street to St. Mary Abbots' was De Maria's restaurant. An advertisement shows it to have been decorated with mermaids supporting the ceiling* but Pound and his friends, who had modest incomes or kept going on odd jobs, could seldom afford to go there. *

The demands made on legs and larynx by the cocktail party were unknown in those days, and most of them had little to spend on alcohol. As Pound added in August 1953, 'it ain't the splendours that make grouping. And booze is not the river of enlightenment.'

Pound and his friends met in a little restaurant in Holland Street, which is still there, having metamorphosed from *White Heather* and *The Old English Rose* to the *Dorothy Plaisance*. For some years the house, built over the site of outbuildings to the old palace, was occupied by Miss Ella Abbott, as Pound wrote:

'Miss Abbott DEFinitely a character/ objected to feeding anyone not connected wiff art or letters/ tho' I suppose some may have got a 1/6 lunch on slim pretensions.

'shd/ think origin rather far S.W. (not the 'MIDDLE' west. which ALL furriners seem to think stretches from Connecticut to the Rockies.)

'anyhow, part of the murkn invasion in search of culture or its vicinity (sd to have flowed from Rice's time in the '70s.)'¹¹

Later Pound added: 'Miss Abbott, American, fleeing from

* When reminded Pound wrote: 'The mermaids had swum thence before 1920.'¹⁰

mid-western desert. Interesting character.' A few months after-wards another memory surfaced. 'Forgot how much I told you re/ Miss Abbott. The flight from U.S.A. toward civilization/ from Mrs John's who fed the whole of Damrosch's orchestra, and housed musicians, to sd/ Miss Abbott who wanted to feed only artists and people who did something at 1/3 per scrambled eggs on one slice of toast.'[12] Pound may have stayed with a lady of this name in New York or had meals in a restaurant fre-quented by members of the American orchestra, which does not appear to have toured Europe until 1920.

Nowadays the same window gives on to Holland Street, filled with cakes made in the kitchen below, and a high skylight over the little tables at the back where coffee and set meals are served. What was probably brown or red wall paper in those days has become cream and maroon paintwork but the walls retain numerous hooks where ornamental plates and various pictures used to hang, of which Whistler's *Mother* and a few watery landscapes have survived.

'Why do we call ourselves Imagists?' Richard Aldington wrote when the group became well known.[13] 'Well, why not? People say "Oh, because it looks silly, and everyone is some sort of an 'ist', and why give yourselves a tag, and what on earth does it mean, and its damn cheek anyway." Well, I think it's a very good descriptive title, and it serves to enumerate some of the principles we most firmly believe in. It cuts us away from the "cosmic" crowd and it equally bars us off from the "abstract art" gang, and it annoys quite a lot of fools. So there you are.'[13]

In *Poetry*, January 1913, there appeared several poems signed 'H.D. Imagiste'. The same issue contained a note by Ezra Pound in which he declared, 'The youngest school here that has the nerve to call itself a school is that of the Imagistes.'

There were a number of enquiries and in March the position was made clear. F. S. Flint, during our talks at Harwell in the 'fifties, thought Imagism a young people's joke, not all that serious. He described how Pound arrived one day with 'an interview with himself' already written but Flint would not sign, so when Pound had left he re-arranged this and sent it back. Pound made further improvements.

'I have it here,' Flint went over to the confusion of books below a window, unsorted since the move from Hampstead, and brought out two pages of typescript, the final article for America. In this Flint had described how he sought out an Imagist 'with intent to discover whether the group itself knew anything about the "movement".'* He discovered they had nothing in common with the Post Impressionists and the Futurists, their only endeavour was to write in accordance with the best tradition as they found it in the best writers of all time—in Sappho, Catullus, Villon. For their own satisfaction they had drawn up a few rules.[14]

(1) Direct treatment of the 'thing', whether subjective or objective.

(2) To use absolutely no word that did not contribute to the presentation.

(3) As regards rhythm, to compose in sequence of the musical phrase, not in sequence of a metronome.

He added that their 'Doctrine of the Image' did not concern the public and would provoke useless discussion.

Flint found among them an earnestness that was amazing to one accustomed to the usual London air of poetic dilettantism. 'They consider that Art is all science, all religion, philosophy and metaphysic. It is true that *snobisme* may be urged against them, but it is at least *snobisme* in its most dynamic form, with a great deal of sound sense and energy behind it, and they are stricter with themselves than with any outsider.'[14]

There followed *A Few Don'ts by an Imagiste*, in which Ezra Pound defined the doctrine. *The New Freewoman* republished both articles, with a note by Rebecca West, who deprecated the Georgian school and then showed that 'there has arisen a little band who desire the poet to be as disciplined and efficient at his job as the stevedore. Just as Taylor and Galbraith want to introduce scientific management into industry, so the Imagistes want to discover the most puissant way of whirling the scattered stardust of words into a new star of passion.'[15]

Pound defined 'an Image' as that which presents 'an intellectual and emotional complex in an instant of time. I use the term 'complex' rather in the technical sense employed by the

---

* Quoted from the article as published in *Poetry*, March 1913. The rules appear in greater detail in *A Retrospect*, *Literary Essays*, p. 3.

newer psychologists, such as Hart, though we might not agree absolutely in our application'.[15]

'It is the presentation of such a "complex" instantaneously which gives that sense of sudden liberation; that sense of sudden growth, which we experience in the presence of the greatest works of art.'[15]

He then goes on to deal with Language, Rhythm and Rhyme and parallels between poetry and music.[15]

As Ford put it, not all who took part treated the movement with reverence. Certain poets were drawn in by the force of Pound's personality. It was necessary for him to have a banner and adherents. Flint and Pound, for instance, were to have some friendly tussles about various aspects later.[16]

Pound, who published the *Des Imagistes* anthology in 1914, never claimed to have originated the movement. It grew from discontents, from a group of younger writers who gradually, by discussion, by the rubbing of edges together came to define their objects.[17] He gave the movement shape and emphasis, got on to paper tendencies already shaping themselves as he reached London. Later Amy Lowell was to take up the term *Imagism* and make a great deal of noise for poetry of her own choice in the U.S.A. As an Irishman put it, ideas are like umbrellas, leave them around, and someone is sure to use them.

11

❊

London and Away

In the summer of 1910 Pound had crossed the Atlantic to visit his parents and see what was happening in America. On board he was reminded of Henry James's view of *The American Scene*, 'the sort of nickel-plate warning which is hurled at one in the saloon of any great transatlantic boat, the awfulness that engulfs one when one comes, for the first time unexpectedly upon a pile of all the *Murkn* [American] magazines laid, shingle-wise, on a brass-studded, screwed-into-place, baise-covered steamer table. The first glitter of the national weapons for driving off quiet and all closer signs of intelligence.'[1] Yet he found that to return to America 'was like going through some very invigorating, very cleansing sort of bath. . . . There may be evil in the country but the odour of rottenness is not obtruded upon one. You meet so many people there who are innocent and unconscious of its existence, so many naive grown children who miss a *double entente*.'[2] *

Yet he could see little hope for the writers. He told Harriet Monroe some time later, 'I may be myopic, but during my last tortured visit to America I found no writer and but one reviewer who had any worthy conception of poetry. The Art!'[3]

Like many another prophet Pound wanted to be accepted by his own people and hoped that eventually there would be a wider cultural development. 'America, my country, is almost a continent and hardly yet a nation, for no nation can be considered historically as such until it has achieved within itself a city to which all roads lead and from which there goes out an authority.'[4]

---

* *Patria Mia* appeared in *The New Age*, 1912, but did not reach book form until 1950. The London edition, 1962, is used here.

'Pin an American down on any fundamental issue you like, and you get—at his last gasp, a quotation.' Pound declared, and pointing out various attributes: 'The contact between the artist and those with whom he must, in the disposal of his work, have contact is, however, so disgusting that I would rather leave it unmentioned.'[4]

No serious work in literature was to be found. Yet at no time was there such machinery for the circulation of printed expression, all favouring a sham; stuff cooked up to suit some editorial palate; yet, within the limits of their comprehension and imagination, the American people themselves did their best. In spite of endowments to Universities and so on, one heard a creaking discontent. 'Hardly a week goes by but I meet or hear of someone who goes into voluntary exile —some reporter who throws up a steady job to come to Europe and breathe; some professor from a freshwater college who comes away on scant savings. Our artists are all over Europe. We do not come away strictly for pleasure. And, we who are constantly railed at as "expatriates", do not hear this with unconcern. We will not put up with it for ever.'[4]

After five years in Europe Pound found great changes in the general atmosphere, the emergence of another period. Architects were bringing a fine spirit of independence to the use of new materials, such as concrete, and he was particularly impressed by the outline of New York. At night the city he had known as a child, seen from a high window, was 'square after square of flame, set and cut into the ether. Here was our poetry, for we have pulled down the stars to our will.'[4]*

As he had done in London and other centres Pound explored like a hunter. 'I see also a sign in the surging crowd on 7th Avenue (New York). A crowd pagan as ever imperial Rome was, eager, careless, with an animal vigour unlike that of any European crowd that I have looked at. There is none of the melancholy, the sullenness, the unhealth of the London mass, none of the worn vivacity of Paris. . . . I do not believe it is in the temper of Vienna. Having been brought up in the American

---

* A poem 'N.Y.', i.e. New York, evidently written at this time, for it first appeared in *Ripostes*, 1912, has been included in *Selected Poems*. It shows the poet in two minds among 'a million people surly with traffic', both loving and hating this city into which he would breathe a soul so that it might live for ever.

medieval system, one returns from Europe and one takes note of
the size and vigour of this new strange people. They are not
Anglo-Saxon, their gods are not the gods whom one was reared
to reverence. And one wonders what they have to do with
lyric measures and the nature of "quantity". One knows that
they are the dominant people and that they are against all
delicate things.'⁴

In September 1912 a loan exhibition of Whistler's work was
held in London, and Pound tells in *Patria Mia* how he had written some bad poetry and burst into several incoherent conversa-
tions trying to explain what it meant to an American. 'I have
taken a deep delight in the novels of Mr Henry James; I have
gathered from Whistler's paintings now at the Tate, more
courage for living than I have gathered from the Canal Bill or
from any other manifest American activity whatsoever.'
Whistler was a man, born American, 'with all our forces of
confusion within him, who has contrived to keep order in his
work, who has attained the highest mastery, and this not by
natural facility but by constant labour and searching.'⁴ Elsewhere he noted the 'peculiarly American passion for "art",
for having a system in things, c.f. Whistler'.⁵

When Pound wrote of the painter in 1912, he must have had
in mind his own difficulties of adjustment to so different an
environment as London at the end of the first decade. Within
Whistler 'were the drawbacks and hindrances at which no
European can more than guess. . . . What Whistler has proved
once and for all, is that being born an American does not eternally damn a man or prevent him from the ultimate and highest
achievement in the arts. And he proved it over many a hindrance
and over many baffled attempts. He is, with Abraham Lincoln,
the beginning of our Great Tradition.'⁶ *

Soon after Pound had arrived in London in 1908 Henry James
had left for America where his brother William James was
seriously ill, and he did not return until 1911. When asked if
he had been down to Lamb House, Rye, Pound replied in 1957,

'Mrs Dilke kindly invited H.J. to lunch one day I was giving
lecture in swank drawingroom pouched† for upkeep by the

---

* See *To Whistler, American*, in *Personae*, 1949.
† Pound was probably paid a fee.

benevolent H. Hewlett [sic] (author of RRRRomantic nuvls,)
Have never been to Rye/ in fact met H.J. only in drawingrooms
of the tolerant.' Later in the same letter, he adds, 'London
possible in 1908 because Browning and H.J., and a few others,
HAD smacked the teak-heads with their flails/ one by one/
driving some sense into 'em. There was in fact a cultural level
above that of the stinkers.'[7]

Two of the social occasions are mentioned in the Pisan
Cantos. In a garden of the Temple, Princess Baryatinskaya*
button-holed the novelist (literally) with the words *Cher Maître*[8]
and elsewhere Henry James was seen trying to escape from a
bore.

> *Mr James shielding himself with Mrs Hawkesby*
> *as it were a bowl shielding itself with a walking stick*
> *as he manoeuvred his way toward the door.'*[9]

When discussing 'national phenomena' Pound wrote elsewhere:

'Men of my time have witnessed "parties" in London
gardens where, as I recall it, everyone else (male) wore grey
"toppers" . . . even Henry James wore one, and unless
memory blends two occasions, he also wore an enormous
checked weskit. Men have witnessed the dinner ceremony on
flagships, where the steward still called it "claret" and bath
oliver appeared with the cheese (Stilton? I suppose it must
have been Stilton.)' Such activities might be called national
phenomena, as opposed to social events which entail an unusual
effort or outlay. Pound then goes on to emphasise, 'I am not
in these slight memories, "pickin' daisies". A man does not
know his own ADDRESS (in time) until he knows where his
time and *milieu* stand in relation to other times and conditions.'[10]

Public indifference to anything in the nature of the arts,
according to Ford, perhaps began with the firing of the first
shot of the Boer War. 'That was the end of everything, of the
pre-Raphaelites, of the Henley gang, of the New Humour, of the
Victorian great figures, of the last traces of the medieval super-

---

* This may have been Lydia Yavorska, a Russian-born actress or Princess
Anatole Marie Baryatinskaya, author of *My Russian Life*, 1921. See *Annotated Index*.
Henry James had a selection of toppers and waistcoats. Pound probably did not
conform.

stition that man might save his soul by the reading of good books.'[11] Not only was there a tremendous increase in the cost of living but London itself was being altered. 'We are the tyrants of the men to come, where we build roads their feet must tread, the traditions we set up, if they are evil, our children will find it hard to fight against; if for want of vigilance we let beautiful places be defiled, it is they who will find it a hopeless task to restore them.'[12]

One street was becoming very like another and this must make a difference to people's psychology. 'You cannot be quite the same man if daily you joggle past St. Mary Abbott's Terrace,' [Kensington High Street] 'on the top of a horse bus; you cannot be quite the same man if you shoot past the terra-cotta plate-glass erections' which replaced the gracious old houses recently demolished. Thoughts must be different, and with each successive blow upon the observation, a person's brain must change a little more. 'And change is all away from the direction of leisure, of spaciousness of thought, of ease.' Each acceleration of a means of access meant more work could be done in a given time, but this was equally true of rivals in business.[13]

'It is a quaint thought,' Ford commented, 'but a perfectly sound one, to say that we are nearer to habits of barbarism, that we could more easily revert to days of savagery than we could pick up again the tone of thought, of mind and habit, of more than thirty years ago.' He concludes with a warning. 'The terra-cotta and plate-glass will inevitably in the course of ages be replaced by swamp, marsh and tidal bed.'[14]

The movement for woman's suffrage had become militant, and Austin Harrison, now editor of *The English Review*, showed that the idea of woman entering public life was disturbing, though she might go into a public house. It was the 'iron Moloch of industry' which forced her into competition with men. Essentially a sign of the times, this unrest ate into the established conditions of people in all countries, 'the inevitable product of an age which is rapidly losing not only faith, but the very hope of faith, and whose need as divinity is money. It is the offspring of socialism, which in turn is the bastard of capitalism.'[15]

In the summer of 1911 there was another war scare: Germany

sent a gunboat to Agadir, and after long negotiations renounced her claims in Morocco in return for concessions in the French Congo.

'Once more Britain was represented in Germany as the arch-enemy of German progress and ambition, and once again as a bar to her overseas policy.'[14] If she wanted a true alliance, argued Austin Harrison, Germany should come to terms about ships, otherwise 'we shall have to go on quietly building ships—two to Germany's every one'.[15]

An unsigned article in *The New Age*, entitled *Money Changers in Literature*, showed that all that had been done in education was to spread out, very thinly, over many, the culture that before was concentrated in a few; there was no cultured class. People paid lip service to the arts, but did not even buy pictures.[16]

'We have to be ready to recognize and if we are strong enough to acclaim that things seeming to us to be hideous may embody a New Beauty,' Ford declared, 'We have to watch modern life sweeping away the traditions that we love, the places we considered hallowed; we have to consider that it is blowing away us ourselves as if we were no more than a little dust. And yet, if we have consciences, we must seek to perceive order in this disorder, beauty in what shocks us, and premonitions of immortality in that which sweeps us into forgotten graves.'[17]

Yet all was not gloom and frustration; the good writer is never welcomed by any community, he must thrust his way up through its indifference, and he is no better off in our own time. Among the books to appear between 1910 and 1912 was Arthur Symons' study of *The Romantic Movement in English Poetry*; Max Beerbohm's *Zuleika Dobson* and *Howards End* by E. M. Forster, then D. H. Lawrence's first novel, *The White Peacock* and over in France the beginning of Proust's *À la Recherche du Temps Perdu*. During the past twelve months, according to *The English Review*, the philosophy of Bergson had been discussed from many points of view.

No one was more aware than Ford, Compton Mackenzie said, of the transformation that literature was undergoing, 'due to the increasing power of machinery and its concomitant the rapid development of megalopolitan culture'.[18] This successful young novelist wrote that too much lyric poetry was a sad lament, but there were signs that it was no longer content to chirp in the golden cage of romance. 'This age has not yet been proved a failure; and if one is sometimes overwhelmed by the contemplation of fled glories, how encouraging it is to stand on the steps of the Albert Memorial, glad to give the Victorians all they had in almost Pharisaic self-congratulation.' For Mackenzie every journey by underground was an Odyssey, there were the personalities of the liftmen; 'waiting on the tempestuous platform—the Cyclopean eye of the advancing train, the adventure of boarding, the fastidiousness in the choice of a neighbour, the sense of equality, the mysterious and flattering reflection of oneself in the opposite windows, even the colours of the various stations—from the orange and lemon of Covent Garden to the bistre melancholy of Caledonian Road or Camden Town, faint cerulean like an autumnal sky.'[18]

Edward Marsh, private secretary to Winston Churchill, then First Lord of the Admiralty, had many literary and artistic friends. He wrote enthusiastically of Rupert Brooke's poems when they first appeared in 1911 and soon was planning with him a collection of the work of the younger poets, to be called the *Georgian Anthology*.

Marsh wrote to Church Walk to ask if certain poems might be included, but Pound regretted this was impossible as he was shortly publishing a further volume. 'Is there anything in the earlier books that you would like? Not *The Goodly Fere* as it doesn't illustrate any *modern* tendency, also I'd like to know more or less in what gallery you propose to put me into? *Canzoni* is the only one that comes within your two year radius. I'm usually in on Tuesday evenings if you'd care to talk over the matter.'[19]

At Church Walk, Marsh explained that unfortunately there was nothing suitable in *Canzoni*. 'Brought together by their friendship for T. E. Hulme, there was no discordant note in their relationship, and Pound, who was to become a severe critic of the later Georgians, courteously expressed a hope that he would one day be represented in their pages.'[19]

A memory from a later phase shows Marsh at one of the Frith Street evenings, sitting on the floor with Rupert Brooke

Industrious John Bullesses

K

and Pound; others there included Middleton Murry, Wilfred Gibson, Wadsworth, Nevinson and Gaudier Brzeska. Hulme also took Marsh to Cambridge to hear Pound read a paper at King's College. At some other time Marsh suggested amendments to a poem shown him by Pound and was somewhat disillusioned to find they had not been used in the final version.[19]

When Pound visited Oxford on one occasion, he met a don who had been in an American University, and spoke of the lists of authors but no books used. There also occurred an incident mentioned several times later and glanced at in *The Cantos*.[20]

'I once met a very ancient Oxford "head", and in the middle of dinner he turned to me, saying: "Ah—um, ah—poet. Ah, some one showed me a new poem the other day, the—ah—the *Hound of Heaven*."'

'I said, "Well, what did you think of it?" and he answered, "Couldn't be bothered to stop for every adjective!"'

'That enlightened opinion was based on a form of comparative literature called "the classic education".'[21]

In another version of the same story Pound adds that one would not have heard this at home, where it would have been accepted from authority as a masterpiece; there would have been no such 'swift and profound censure, that scrap of criticism which touches the root and seed of Thompson's every effort'.[22]

According to Virginia Woolf, the Post-Impressionist Exhibition of 1910 had thrown the public 'into paroxysms of rage and laughter. They went from Cézanne to Gauguin, from Gauguin to Van Gogh, they went from Picasso to Segonzac, from Derain to Friez, and they were infuriated.'[23] The younger artists looked to Roger Fry for leadership, and followed his idea that one should accept modern conditions and make the best of them. A second Exhibition in 1912 included the work of a number of English painters still almost unknown, among them Wyndham Lewis, Eric Gill and Stanley Spencer.

Writing in *The English Review*, Walter Sickert declared that it was almost a quarter of a century since he had ranged himself, to his own satisfaction, definitely against the Whistlerian anti-literary theory of drawing. Now 'Mr. Fry's earth-shaking jumble at the Grafton Gallery, where everything was booked

At the Ballet

through, like the luggage of a travelling company, as Post-Impressionism', was over. 'The cubical, conical, cylindrical, rhomboidal invasion' had been routed, 'and everything, as they say in France, has re-entered into order. The only lady-fauviste in the country is reported to have taken the night boat to Montmartre, disguised in a thick blue outline, and students are back on their stools continuing to study drawing.'[24]

The Russian Ballet, under the direction of Diaghilev, had also made people feel that the decade before them was to provide a great expansion in the arts. Pound of course, was interested and he may have become friendly with Serafima Astafieva, who later opened a school in London; certainly one image of her as she stood inside the street doors of the Wigmore Hall, remained in his mind for many years.[25]

The English Review for August 1911, had carried an unsigned sketch on the new art which had conquered Russia, Berlin, Paris and now London. It had been provided by an Englishman, Gordon Craig, son of Ellen Terry, 'The Lady Diana, who was a very grand person in Society,' looked up the meaning of the word 'choreography' and took a party to the Russian ballet. ' "It's something new," she said, "choreography they call it but personally I think this Cleopatra ballet rather tiresome".' And her friends mostly agreed. One person defended the work and pointed out that the neglect of Augustus John's portraits for those of the academic painters emphasised a general disregard for the arts. ' "I don't understand." And the Lady Diana turned upon him her famous Luini smile.'[26]

Gordon Craig's *Art of the Theatre* was also reviewed that year. He had declared himself more miserable than ever before in realising the 'hopeless inactivity of England and our stage . . . the utter stupidity of everyone connected with the Arts in England, the death-like complacency with which London thinks it is active and intelligent in these matters, the idiocy of that section of the press which calls every courageous attempt to revive life and art "eccentric", that lack of companionship in London, that best for two-pence at all costs.'[27]

12

---✳---

Innovations

Pound compared London to a great and if you like, un-
serious picture-book, and its pages were of infinite
variety. 'There is no week without some new thing of
interest, no fortnight in which some new and interesting personality is not whirled up against one.[1] It was like Rome of
the decadence, all the prominent writers were from other
countries, Yeats, James, Hudson and Conrad. Wells and
Bennett combined vigour with consummate vulgarity, the
bubbling of G. K. Chesterton making a poor second to the
bellowing of Belloc.

'Perched on the dry rim of the cauldron' were all the naive
transpontine observers, the 'British institutions, Gosse, Garnett and their penumbra, the powers of the world of letters,
with Hampstead as a more hideous sort of Boston. . . . A month
ago there was a great poet from Bengal [Rabindranath Tagore],
three weeks ago it was a renovator of an art that is almost
new, three days ago it was some one en passant whose name I
scarcely caught—the continuous torrent process. These people
carry you particles of knowledge and gossip, wearing you away
little by little, filing against your salients. And this process
becomes so much the usual, the dull and accustomed, that one
forgets that the city ever had a lure and a mystery. All this
sounds sadly like sentiment or rhetoric. And I dare say it is,
so I end it.'[1]

It was not surprising that the 'institutions' resented Pound.
'All this throwing down of fire-irons and sputtering of four-
letter words is merely Ezra's form of defence against a not too
considerate world,' Richard Aldington wrote. 'In 1912 he was
great fun, a small but persistent volcano in the dim levels of

London literary society, London was interested and amused by him.'²

John Cournos, himself of Russian origin, found that compared with the Englishman, Pound was a glasshouse, with all the furnishings of his mind visible. Always ready to help with translations into English, he found him 'the kindest man that ever lived', and without a trace of malice.³

In *The New Age* emphasis was laid on the ugliness of misapplied wealth 'while artists devour their hearts in bitterness, the people of London live amid squalor so immense, so wide . . . yet all the offence to the eye has not killed the spirit'. The vulgar rich were the enemies of the artist.⁴ Pound had seen two things in London that could compare to nothing but Kipling's sea monster.

'Once in Regent Street, going towards Oxford Circus. It had lost a leg, from the knees. It must have been fresh from the hospital, for the cicatrice was still red. It must have had on the clothing worn at the time of the accident, for the breeches were torn and showed the surgeon's job. The other in Oxford Street, near Hyde Park. It was compact and beer fed and sore-eyed and nearly blind with hunger.'⁵

'These hulks were no worse to look at than many others, but they were striking in this, that they were not inert . . . not Verhaeren's *Pauvres Gens aux Gestes las et indulgents*. The first moved swiftly, with great swings between its clumsy crutches, the second apparently slowly yet with a recklessness that marked its movement from that of anything else in the crowd about the bus-stop. The legs moved stiff from the hips, with no bend at knee or ankle. Each of these things moved in rhythm regular as a metronome, moved by a force as unreasoning as that of a tree or a flood. The first was young, the second over forty. Neither looked to right nor left. They neither asked nor gave one time to offer them alms. They made no protest.'⁵

'I think that only this twice in my life have I seen bodies so completely gripped by the will.

' "Of course one can't prevent . . .".

'I don't wish to prevent anything. I am not a humanitarian but a humanist. The drama (?) of life depends on inequalities. Let us maintain them? No. They will maintain themselves without our meagre assistance.'⁵

On October 22nd, 1913, Alvin Langdon Coburn went to ten Church Walk to photograph Ezra Pound. 'In those days one carried a lot of paraphernalia about, and while I was fixing it Ezra kept up his usual good talk, about books and art, all he was interested in'.

Mrs. W. B. Yeats has drawn attention to the fact that Pound posed in his dressing gown as he was recovering from an attack of jaundice, which perhaps accounts for the Renaissance effect. Pound was very pleased with the portrait, which was to be used in *Lustra*. It would make the junior typists 'clasp their hand ecstatically'. Or as Yeats says, '*That'll* sell the book.' Mrs. Langley remarked, 'Oh, the first that ever did you justice.' Then at the doorway, depreciatingly, 'Eh. I hope you won't be offended sir, but, eh, It-is-like-the-good-man-Nazereth, isn't it sir?'

'For one man I strike there are ten to strike back at me. I stand exposed . . .'

Pound then formulates some ideas on practical education and mentions American attempts to clear the slums and how the Jews, 'this wise and provident people' put their children to trades. Over there he had watched the slum children using trams to reach the parks. 'Very instructive to watch this kind of straw.'[5]

Arthur Thorn also protested against the inadequacy of institutions for the blind and the indifference of the public to their condition. 'All day long she sits in her old bath chair holding in her transparent hand matches, laces, studs. I have missed many home-going trams watching her. . . . Young, and obviously in the last stages of consumption, her blind father sits beside her on a stool reading from a braille Testament but his voice is drowned by the noise of heavy traffic . . . the words of life fall only on his and his daughter's ears. Each time I pass I expect to see him sitting alone, with head a little lower bowed, passing his hands wearily over the raised type, mumbling the words of Christ.'[6]

In 1911 Pound was in Paris, where he became friendly with the musician Walter Rummel, with whom he was to collaborate later. Perhaps his interest in Remy de Gourmont and other contemporary French writers dates from this visit. In the summer Pound was also in Italy with Mrs. Shakespear and her daughter, and they probably went to Verona, with its soft pink sandstone buildings and the signed pillars in the beautiful church of San Zeno which so impressed Pound. Then there were the paintings of Pisanello in the gallery along the river—had Pound already seen his work in the Tempio Malatestiano in Rimini?

If the ladies had not been to Sirmione before he could act as guide to this long nib-shaped piece of rock, almost an island with its moated castle known to Dante, part of the area incrusted with villas and streets and garden walls. Away at the end, beyond the church of San Pietro in Mavino, with its old, time-softened frescoes and deep cool after the dry warmth outside, the olive trees surround the grotto of Catullus.

Instead of discussing the art of poetry, Pound once said, he would much rather 'lie on what is left of Catullus' parlour floor and speculate the pure azure beneath it and the hills off Salo and Riva with their forgotten gods moving unhindered amongst them'.[7] A poem in *Exultations* suggests this or a similar experience:

> ... If at Sirmio,
> My soul I meet thee, when this life's outrun,
> Will we not find some headland consecrated
> By aery apostles of terrene delight,
> Will not our cult be founded on the waves,
> Clear sapphire, cobalt, cyanine,
> On triune azures, the impalpable
> Mirrors unstill of the eternal change?
> Soul, if She meet us there, will any rumour
> Of havens more high and courts desirable
> Lure us beyond the cloudy peak of Riva?[8]

It is there again in the Cantos, expressed with a directness which it has taken a lifetime to achieve:

> Lay in soft grass by the cliff's edge
> with the sea 30 metres below this
>   and at hand's span, at cubit's reach moving,
> the crystalline, as inverse of water,
>   clear over rock-bed[9]

There follows a description of the 'gemmed field' but such a moment, however long remembered, is not yet *atasal*—union with God.

Then there was an evening, at the other side of the lake, when the mountains were Japanese in outline, 'as Fujiyama at Gardone' and a cat walked the top bar of the railing, 'in the stillness outlasting all wars'. Each man there seemed contained by his own recollections until one of them spoke:

> 'La Donna,' said Nicoletti
>   la donna,
>   la donna![10] *

That spring W. B. Yeats had also been in Paris and Pound wrote to his father. 'Yeats I like very much. I've seen him a great deal, almost daily. . . . He is, as I have said before, a very great man, and he improves on acquaintance.'[11] Back in

---

* The passage has several echoes in other parts of the cantos, perhaps to suggest a question which has never been fully answered.

London Yeats listened with interest and some amusement to the doings of the loosely-knit group of American and English writers calling themselves Imagists, but he did not wholly accept their sweeping condemnation, their youthfully emphatic doctrines. 'We older writers disliked this new poetry,' he said, 'but were forced to admit its satiric intensity.'[12]

Comments on Yeats' own poetry were becoming less enthusiastic and the poet himself was tired of theatre business and 'the management of men'. 'All spontaneous joy and natural content' had disappeared. As he looked back, 'my generation, because it disliked rhetorical, moral flavour, came to dislike all rhetoric. . . . Here and there some young revolutionist would boast that his eyes were on the present or the future, or even denounce all poetry back to Dante, but we were content; we wrote as men had always written.'[12] Yet a change was preparing itself even earlier; when he came to know Synge's work Yeats realized that the poet must denounce, as he noted in 1909, 'the deliberate creation of a kind of Holy City of the imagination, and express the individual'.[13] 'When I came to London I found a group of young lyric writers who were also against rhetoric. We formed the Rhymers' Club. . . . We wanted to get rid not only of rhetoric but of poetic diction. We tried to strip away everything that was artificial, to get a style like speech, as simple as the simplest prose, like a cry of the heart.'[14]

'We rebelled against rhetoric and now there is a group of younger poets who dare to call us rhetorical. When I returned to London from Ireland, I had a young man go over all my work with me to eliminate the abstract. This was the American poet Ezra Pound.'[14]

Evidently Yeats did not take exception to the note which Pound dated London, December 10th 1912 and sent to *Poetry*. 'The state of things here in London as I see it, is as follows: I find Mr Yeats the only poet worthy of serious study. . . . As to his English contemporaries, they are food, sometimes very good food for anthologies. There are a number of men who have written a poem, or several poems, worth knowing and remembering, but they do not much concern the young artist studying the art of poetry.'[15] The important work of the past twenty-five years had been done in Paris. There had been imitations of the French poets but little serious consideration of their *method*. 'I would rather talk about poetry with Ford Madox Hueffer than with any man in London.' His beliefs were in diametric opposition to those of Yeats, who has been subjective and believed in the glamour and associations which hang near the words; and evidently quoting him, '"Works of art beget works of art."' He had much in common with the French symbolists whereas Ford, who had his origins in Gautier or in Flaubert, would strip words of all 'associations' for the sake of getting a precise meaning. Yeats' gifts to English art were mostly negative; he had stripped English poetry of many of its faults. One school tended to lapse into sentiment, the other to become descriptive. The watchword of the Imagist was precision.[15]

On another occasion Pound said that Ford had hammered his point of view into him, meeting with little resistance. 'When one really feels and thinks, one stammers with a simple speech. It is only in the flurry, the shallow frothy excitement of writing or the inebriety of a metre, that one falls into the easy, easy, oh so easy speech of books and poems one has read.'[16]

It was said that Pound altered some of Yeats' poems before sending them to *Poetry* but in fact he made suggestions and noted on a typescript to the present writer 'very few'.[17]

Yeats, unmarried and nearing fifty, needed a settled background, but although he now had a small pension from the Civil List he was by no means well off. Digestive troubles, headaches and continual worry with his eyes affected him during the winter of 1912 to 1913. 'His life at Woburn Buildings was only rendered tolerable by the assiduous attentions of Ezra Pound who would come to read to him in the evening and also helped him to health by teaching him to fence.'[18] Later Yeats told Lady Gregory, 'Ezra never shrinks from work. A learned companion and a pleasant one, he is full of the Middle Ages and helps me to get back to the more definite and concrete, away from modern abstractions; to talk over a poem with him is like getting you to put a sentence into dialect. All becomes clear and natural. Yet in his own work he is very uncertain, often very bad though very interesting sometimes. He spoils himself by too many experiments and has more sound principles than taste.'[19]

At that time Yeats complained of his huge mail and Pound probably helped to answer this 'daily plague'. When Yeats' papers came to be sorted many years later, Pound's writing was on a number of envelopes containing drafts he had gathered together and which might otherwise have been lost.[20]

'I think he learned the proper treatment of modern subjects before I did.'[21] Pound was writing of D. H. Lawrence, whose poem *Snapdragon* appeared shoulder to shoulder with *The Return*, in *The English Review* for June 1912. The contrast in style is clearly shown there. That autumn Pound was correcting proofs of another volume, the fourth in three years, called *Ripostes*, probably from a fencing term meaning counter-blows. At the end were poems by T. E. Hulme, presented for 'good fellowship' and seeing 'that they recall certain evenings and meetings of two years gone, dull enough at the time, but rather pleasant to look back upon'.[22]

The first thrust was given to 'the worthiest of editors' whose mind, made up in the 'seventies, worked to represent:

> .   .   .   *that school of thought*
> *Which brought the hair-cloth chair to such perfection,*
> *Nor will the horrid threats of Bernard Shaw*
> *Shake up the stagnant pool of its convictions*:[23]

There were poems with a classical or Egyptian background, several arising from pictures; also *The Virginal* with its suggestion of earlier English or perhaps Provençal rhythms, in contrast to direct love-making themes such as *A Girl* and *The Needle*. *The Seafarer*, from the Anglo-Saxon, and others, have passed into later collections. Pound himself was not altogether satisfied, for he wrote three years later; 'Nineteen twelve was a bad year, we all ran about like puppies with tin cans tied to our tails. The tin cans of Swinburne, rhyming Browningisms, even in Mr Ford's case, of Kiplingisms.'[24]

F. S. Flint had realised much earlier, that in spite of their uncertainties in places, Pound's two previous volumes had proved that the old devices of regular metrical beat and regular rhyming were worn out, and that, 'The poet must forge his own rhythm according to the impulse of the creative emotion working through him.'[25] He quotes William Watson's criticism of 'You phrase-tormenting fantastic chorus, with strangest words at your beck and call.'

Innovations

You prance on language, you force, you strain it,
You rack and you rive it, you twist it and maul,
Form you abhor it and taste, you disdain it.
And here was a bard shall outlast you all.[25] *

Jean de Bosschère found that between *Ripostes* and the next phase of Pound's work, the poet 'has had a revelation. He sees the world in harder outline, its grin is changed. . . . The value of *Ripostes* lies in the poet's point of view. His style is formed. He awaits a shock. . . . He seems, having got his strength, to put away the old harmonies of poetry, so well, too well, known to us.'[26]

All writers want magazines in which they and their friends can see themselves in print. Orage could not take all that Pound proposed and the space given to poetry was necessarily limited. In the summer of 1912 Pound offered to help Harriet Monroe with *Poetry*. 'This forlorn hope was started in Chicago about a year and a half ago,' Pound wrote, 'and in the dark occidental continent its editress raised the quixotic standard. "We intend to print the best poetry being written in English." And the odd thing is that this provincial paper should, to some extent, have done it. . . . It is also safe to say that they print more important poems than all the rest of the American magazines put together.'[27] He told her he would try and teach the American poet 'that poetry *is* an art, an *art* with a technique, with media, and an art which must be in constant flux, a constant change of manner if it is to live'.[28]

In London he knew nearly everyone who mattered and would send her poems by W. B. Yeats, 'H.D.', Richard Aldington and 'the very great Bengali poet whose work is going to be the sensation of the winter, Rabindranath Tagore'.[29] He also related how Arthur Quiller-Couch had asked if he might publish some of his poems in *The Oxford Book of Victorian Verse* but had chosen those which Pound had decided not to republish. As he heard no further he presumed 'this is what happens if you've a plymouth-rock conscience landed on a predilection for the arts'.[30] In fact two poems were included.

Those who had not come to know and like Pound or who listened to the inevitable legends which accompany those who

---

* i.e. Alfred Lord Tennyson, 1809–92.

disrupt the fish-pond of London life, were annoyed by his out-spokenness. At one point he tells Harriet Monroe that he was making three enemies in a line, 'for one man I strike there are ten to strike back at me. I stand exposed. It hits me in my dinner invitations, in my weekends, in reviews of my own work. Nevertheless it's a good fight.'[30]

In *Poetry* for May 1914 there appeared the first of Ernest Fenollosa's transcriptions from the Japanese, arranged by Pound, who wrote in *The Egoist* for June 1st, 1914, under another name: 'It is beginning to be whispered that Fenollosa was one of the most important men of his time: that he was part in some way, of a sort of obscure renaissance; that his work on Chinese and Japanese art was only a part of what he accomplished as Imperial Commissioner for Arts in Japan. It is known that he left a great mass of manuscripts relating to Chinese and Japanese verse.'

Pound was soon publishing his *Contemporanea* in *Poetry*, April 1913. Earlier the poet had conversed with his own songs, comparing them to rain drops falling on a sullen sea, and now as deer mating with their own kind: he warns them of hostilities from the 'generation of the thoroughly smug and thoroughly uncomfortable'[31] who will flee from them in horror. In 'Salutation the Second' the poet declares:

> *You were praised my books,*
> *   because I had just come from the country:*
> *I was twenty years behind the times*
> *   so you found an audience ready.*
> *I do not disown you,*
> *   do not you disown your progeny.*
>
> *Here they stand without quaint devices,*
> *Here they are with nothing archaic about them,*
> *Watch the reporters spit, watch the grin of the professors,*
> *Watch how the pretty ladies revile them:* *
>
> *'Is this' they say, 'the nonsense*
> *   that we expect of poets?'*
> *'Where is the Picturesque?'*

---

* Later these last three lines became 'Observe the irritation in general', in *Selected Poems*.

'Where is the vertigo of emotion?'
'No! His first work was the best.'
'Poor dear! He has lost his illusions.'[32]

The Condolence begins, 'O my fellow sufferers, songs of my youth,/ A lot of asses praise you because you are "virile",' and concludes by showing that 'We are compared to that sort of person/ Who wanders about announcing his sex/ As if he had just discovered it./ Let us leave this matter, my songs,/ and return to that which concerns us.'[33] In *Exultations*, de Bosschère noted later, 'the virile note' sounded 'with strange and rather crude strength and even then 'the poet was reproached for it'.[34] Although his poems hardly seem very startling now, Pound was to meet more and more criticism on both sides of the Atlantic. After the publication of *To Whistler, American*, Harriet Monroe commented in *Poetry*:

'Apparently we of "these States" have no longing for an Ezekiel; our prophets must give us, not the bitter medicine that we need, but the sugar-and-water of compliment which we can always swallow with a smile. . . . Mr Pound is not the first American poet who has stood with his back to the wall, and struck out blindly with clenched fists in a fierce impulse to fight. Nor is he the first whom we, by this same stolid and indifferent rejection, have forced into exile and rebellion.'[35]

Pound was to write a poem which was initially called *Lustra* and then became *The Rest*.

> *O helpless few in my country,*
> *O remnant enslaved! . . .*
>
> *Take thought:*
> *I have weathered the storm,*
> *I have beaten out my exile.*[36]

POSTSCRIPT

'GET IT. Dig it.' Pound urged. As the material for an account of his background accumulated, I began to feel like the Hen in *Finnegans Wake* scratching through the rubbish heaps of the past for significant detail. There was so much that it seemed almost impossible to make it book-shape. Therefore it is best to pause here, at the end of Pound's first years in England.

A number of other people he had known in Kensington and elsewhere were mentioned in his letters to me but each requires a 'biographic "fiche"' and this is slow work. Pound's journalism, the use of Fenollosa's manuscripts, and the publication of *Cathay*, *Lustra* and other books, the early Cantos and *Hugh Selwyn Mauberley* must also come under a further title.

To reach the later Cantos, where so much of Kensington is remembered, it will be necessary to summarise the intervening phases, in Paris, Rapallo and Rome, and to mention Pound's detention in the United States.

'The essential thing in a poet is that he builds us his world.' Pound was writing in 1915,[1] long before André Billy had reached a similar conclusion. 'You can forgive a poet his sins for the sake of his virtues, "because he hath loved much". But it is a consummate slovenliness of general criticism to see no flaw in the idol merely because *numen inest*.'

Notes

Unless indicated all publications are British. In most cases where Pound's articles have been reprinted, the recent source is given. Where there is no index or a reference is hard to trace, page numbers are included. Pound's criticism has been considerably compressed to give some idea of his development and methods, so that the reader unfamiliar with his work is advised to consult the originals. Unfortunately it has not been possible to deal with Pound's interest in Turkish affairs during the early years in London.

E.P.	Ezra Pound.
Cantos	*The Cantos of Ezra Pound*, Faber, 1964.
Selected Poems	*The Selected Poems of Ezra Pound*, with an introduction by T. S. Eliot. Faber, 1933. Frequently re-issued.
Letters	*The Letters of Ezra Pound*, 1907–1941. Edited D. D. Paige. Faber, 1951.
Lit. Essays	*The Literary Essays of Ezra Pound*, Faber, 1954. Paperback, 1960.
G. to K.	*Guide to Kulchur*, Ezra Pound, Faber, 1938.
Pavannes	*Pavannes and Divagations*. Peter Owen, 1960.
Rome Broadcasts	*Ezra Pound Broadcasts*. Federal Communications Commission, U.S.A. Microfilm in the British Museum, of short-wave broadcasts, 1941–3.
E.P. to P.H.	Letters written by Ezra Pound to Patricia Hutchins.
Annotated Index	*Annotated Index to the Cantos of Ezra Pound*, I–LXXXIV, by J. H. Edwards. California, 1959.

NOTES

Quotation on p. 11, *A Visiting Card*, Ezra Pound, 1952, p. 30.

Introductions

1. Unpublished letter from T. S. Eliot to James Joyce, June 1923. See *James Joyce's World*, Patricia Hutchins, 1957, p. 143

2. *American Literature and the American Language*, T. S. Eliot, St. Louis, 1953

3. *Hugh Selwyn Mauberley*, *Selected Poems*

4. *The Poetry of Ezra Pound*, Hugh Kenner, 1951, which includes 'This Hulme Business' by E.P.

5. *A Portrait of the Artist as a Young Man*, James Joyce

6. Introduction by T. S. Eliot in *Lit. Essays*

7. *The Garden, Selected Poems*

8. To P.H., June 26, 1953

9. To P.H., October 30, 1957

10. To P.H., August 18, 1957

11. To P.H., June 5, 1957

12. *A Visiting Card*, E.P., 1952, p. 30

13. G. to K., p. 84

14. *Egoist*, February 2, 1914

15. To P.H., November 2, 1957

16. To P.H., December 21, 1956

17. To P.H., May 3, 1957

18. To P.H., December 21, 1956

19. Canto 74, p. 459

20. To P.H., March 1, 1957

21. *L'Epoque 1900*, 1885–1905 André Billy, Paris, 1951

22. *Poetry*, Chicago, June 1915, p. 140

Chapter One. Backgrounds—British and American

1. *Letters*, p. 446

2. *New Age, The Revolt of Intelligence*, E.P., January 8, 1920

3. *Dictionary of English Surnames*, Reaney, 1958. Also *English and Welsh Surnames*, Bardsley, 1901

4. *Egoist*, September 1918, p. 107

5. *Twentieth Century Authors*, Kuntz and Haycraft, 1942

6. *Indiscretions or une revue de deux mondes*, E.P., first appeared in the *New Age*, 1920, now in *Pavannes*, p. 50

7. To P.H., August 1953

8. Further details are in *Ezra Pound*, Charles Norman, New York, 1960

9. *Pavannes*, p. 11

10. Norman

11. Norman

12. *Pavannes*, p. 25

13. *New Age, The Regional*, E.P., October 9, 1919

14. *Pavannes*, p. 40

15. Old Testament. *Ezra*, Chap. 10

16. *Tristram Shandy*, Laurence Sterne

17. *From the Life*, Phyllis Bottome, 1946, p. 76

18. *Pavannes*, p. 41

19. *Pavannes*, p. 41

20. *Oxford Companion to English Literature,* 3rd edition
21. *Letters,* p. 121
22. *Pavannes,* p. 43
23. Norman
24. *Lit. Essays,* p. 303
25. *Lit. Essays,* p. 296
26. *Pavannes,* pp. 47–8
27. *New Age, The Regional,* E.P., November 13, 1919
28. Rome Broadcasts, May 9, 1942
29. *Lit. Essays,* p. 383
30. Canto 77, p. 495
31. G. to K., p. 145
32. *Annotated Index . . .* and Norman
33. Canto 80, p. 547
34. *Letters,* p. 157

35. *New Age, The Regional,* E.P., October 9, 1919
36. *Pavannes,* pp. 45–6.
37. *I wanted to write a poem,* William Carlos Williams, Boston, 1958
38. *Selected Letters,* William Carlos Williams, N.Y., 1947. As quoted by Norman
39. *I wanted to write a poem,* Williams
40. *Autobiography,* William Carlos Williams, U.S.A., 1945
41. Rome Broadcasts, May 9, 1942
42. *Autobiography,* Williams
43. Quoted by Norman; no source
44. To P.H. in conversation

Chapter Two. Europe—Provence and Italy

1. To P.H., November 2, 1957
2. *A Visiting Card,* E.P., 1952, p. 21
3. To P.H., April 10, 1958
4. Norman
5. Norman
6. Canto 74, p. 474, and Canto 80, p. 550
7. G. to K., p. 219
8. See Canto 3, p. 15
9. *New Age, America: Chances and Remedies,* E.P., May 8, 1913
10. Norman
11. *Selected Poems*
12. *Letters,* p. 38
13. *Letters,* p. 41
14. To P.H., February 9, 1958
15. Canto 80, p. 533
16. *Pavannes,* p. 18, p. 9
17. Canto 84, p. 574
18. *Pavannes,* p. 5
19. *Lit. Essays. Troubadours—*

Their Sorts and Conditions, p. 101
20. *T.P.'s Weekly. How I began* E.P., June 1913
21. *Lit. Essays. Troubadours,* etc., p. 101
22. *Cino, Selected Poems*
23. *Provencia Deserta, Selected Poems*
24. Canto 20, p. 93
25. *New Age, Provincialism the Enemy,* E.P., July 26, 1917
26. Canto 80, p. 546
27. To P.H., May 3, 1957
28. *Pavannes*
29. To P.H., February 8, 1958
30. *Selected Poems*
31. Canto 26, p. 126
32. Canto 3, p. 15
33. Canto 84, p. 489.
34. *Ezra Pound, his Metric and Poetry,* U.S.A., 1917. T. S. Eliot

Notes

1. Rome Broadcasts, May 5, 1942

2. As above

3. *Letters*, p. 229

4. *T.P.'s Weekly. How I began*, E.P., June 1913

5. To P.H. on tss.

6. *Letters*, p. 40

7. *Letters*, p. 146

8. *A Lume Spento*, E.P., Venice, 1908

9. To P.H., November 28, 1956

10. *Letters*, pp. 36–40

11. *Ancient Lights*, Ford Madox Hueffer, 1911, p. 270

12. Rome Broadcasts, March 19, 1942

13. *The Soul of London*, Ford Madox Hueffer, 1905

14. *English Review*, December 1908, p. 162

15. *The Soul of London*

16. *Ancient Lights*, p. 288

17. *T.P.'s Weekly. How I began*, etc.

18. *Personae*, E.P., 1909

19. *New Age*, June 1908

20. *Provence*, Ford Madox Ford, 1938, p. 54

21. *Ancient Lights*, p. 223

22. *The Last Pre-Raphaelite*, Goldring, 1948, pp. 89–90

23. *The March of Literature*, F. M. Ford, U.S.A., 1939, p. 717

24. *The Last Pre-Raphaelite*

25. *New English Weekly*, November 8, 1939

26. London P.O. Directory, 1909. See Canto 80, p. 536

27. To P.H., March 28, 1958

28. *Letters*, p. 144

29. *T.P.'s Weekly*, etc.

30. *Exile's Return*, Malcolm Cowley, 1961

31. *T.P.'s Weekly*, etc.

32. In conversation with P.H.

33. *New Age*, January 1913

34. To P.H., December 1, 1953

35. To P.H., November 29, 1956

36. To P.H., March 28, 1953

37. *The Invisible Poet*, Kenner, 1960, p. 87

38. To P.H., April 7, 1954

39. *Ezra Pound*, T. S. Eliot

40. *English Hours*, Henry James, 1960, p. 79

41. To P.H., May 7, 1957

42. To P.H. in conversation

43. *Letters*, p. 107

44. *Letters*, p. 41

45. Unpublished letter by E.P. to Mrs. Elkin Mathews

46. Canto 82, p. 558

47. Phyllis Bottome in conversation with P.H.

48. *Memoirs of an Edwardian*, Edgar Jepson, 1937, p. 152

49. *New Age*, May 27, 1909

50. *Selected Poems*

51. *Letters*, p. 41

52. *Times Literary Supplement*, August 26, 1909

53. *T.P.'s Weekly*, etc.

54. *Selected Poems*

55. *Personae*

Notes

Chapter Four. Church Walk, Kensington

1. B.B.C. Recording by E.P., 1960
2. A descendant to P.H.
3. *Letters*, p. 149
4. To P.H., October 30, 1953
5. To P.H., July 20, 1957
6. To P.H., September 18, 1957
7. To P.H., October 30, 1953
8. To P.H., September 19, 1953
9. To P.H., September 27, 1957
10. To P.H., September 27, 1957
11. To P.H., September 19, 1953
12. To P.H., September 27, 1957
13. *Some Went This Way*, R. F. Seymour, Chicago, 1945
14. *Death of a Hero*, Richard Aldington, 1930
15. To P.H., November 14, 1957
16. *The Bathtub, Selected Poems*
17. *It was the Nightingale*, Ford, 1934, p. 34
18. To P.H., February 8, 1958.
19. Canto 80, p. 542
20. To P.H., December 1, 1953
21. E.P. on tss. by P.H.
22. *London Town, Past and Present*, W. Hutchings, 1909. Contribution by Ford Madox Hueffer, Vol. 2, p. 752
23. Canto 74, p. 461
24. Canto 80, p. 551

Chapter Five. The Spirit of Romance

1. *Philadelphia Evening Bulletin*, February 20, 1928, as quoted by Norman
2. To P.H. in conversation
3. *The Spirit of Romance*, Ezra Pound, M.A., 1910. Revised edition of 1953 used here
4. To P.H., September 19, 1953
5. *Spirit of Romance*
6. *Spirit of Romance*. Postscript to edition of 1929
7. *New Age. I gather the limbs of Osiris* series, E.P., December 7, 1911
8. *Spirit of Romance*, p. 22
9. *Spirit of Romance*, p. 88
10. *English Review*, July 1910
11. *The Poetry of Ezra Pound*, Hugh Kenner, 1951, p. 337
12. *Poetry Review*, January 1912
13. *New Age, Osiris* series, December 7, 1911
14. *New Age, Osiris* series, December 14, 1911
15. *The Sonnets and Ballate of Guido Cavalcanti*, E.P., 1912
16. *English Review*, July 1912
17. *Times Literary Supplement*, November 21, 1912
18. *Times Literary Supplement*, December 6, 1912
19. *The Sonnets*, also *The Translations* of Ezra Pound, 1953
20. *Patria Mia*, E.P., published serially in the *New Age* from September 1912. In book form, Chicago, 1950, p. 39
21. Canto 80, p. 541
22. *Egoist*, October 1, 1914

23. *Patria Mia*
24. *Lit. Essays*, p. 111
25. *Spirit of Romance*, pp. 87–94
26. *Egoist*, April 1, 1914
27. *Egoist*, March 1, 1916
28. *New Age, Provincialism the Enemy*, E.P., July 19, 1917
29. G. to K., p. 300
30. To P.H., November 29, 1956
31. *New Age*, December 21, 1911
32. To P.H., August 1956
33. *Letters of W. B. Yeats*, 1954, p. 543
34. *The Poetry of Ezra Pound*, Hugh Kenner, p. 307
35. *W. B. Yeats*, J. M. Hone, 1943
36. *Ezra Pound*, edited Peter Russell, 1950
37. *W. B. Yeats*, Hone, p. 281
38. Harriet Shaw Weaver in conversation with P.H.
39. Canto 82, p. 559
40. Quoted by J. M. Hone in *W. B. Yeats*
41. *Autobiography*, William Carlos Williams

Chapter Six. Holland Park Avenue

1. *New Freewoman*, September 15, 1913
2. Quoted in *The Last Pre-Raphaelite*, p. 194
3. *English Review*, December 1908
4. *The Critical Attitude*, Hueffer, 1911, p. 29
5. *New Freewoman*, September 5, 1913
6. For these and further details see *South Lodge*, 1943, and *The Last Pre-Raphaelite*, 1948, both by Douglas Goldring
7. *The Flurried Years*, Violet Hunt, 1926
8. *South Lodge*
9. *Rude Assignment*, Wyndham Lewis, 1930, p. 121
10. *Rude Assignment*, p. 122
11. *Letters of Wyndham Lewis*, edited W. R. Rose, 1963
12. *Rude Assignment*, p. 110
13. *Blasting and Bombardiering*, Wyndham Lewis, 1937
14. Canto 80, p. 541
15. *Blasting*, etc., p. 279
16. *Blasting*, etc., p. 277
17. *Poetry*, January 1913, p. 127
18. *Letters from Limbo*, Ernest Rhys, 1940, p. 12
19. To P.H., December 2, 1956
20. *Wales England Wed*, Ernest Rhys, 1940, p. 177
21. *Everyman Remembers*, Ernest Rhys, 1931, pp. 251–4
22. To P.H. in conversation
23. *Everyman Remembers*, as above
24. To P.H., August 18, 1957
25. *New Age*, August 29, 1908
26. *English Review*, August 1909
27. *Annual Register*, 1908, 1909
28. *English Review*, August, 1909, p. 140
29. *Egoist, Suffragettes*, E.P., July 1, 1914

Notes

30. E.P. to P.H. on tss. of notes

31. *English Review*, January 1910

32. *New Age*, May 1911

33. *George V*, Harold Nicolson, 1952, p. 156

34. *New Age*, January 1911

35. *The Condition of England*, C. F. G. Masterman, 1909, p. 1

36. *English Review*, August 1910

37. Masterman, pp. 260, 360, 232

38. *Selected Poems*

Chapter Seven. Cursitor Street

1. *English Review*, September 1909, p. 318

2. Kenner, p. 308

3. *English Review*, November 1909, p. 671. Also see:

4. *The Critical Attitude*, Hueffer, p. 184 and p. 110

5. To P.H., May 10, 1957

6. To P.H., February 8, 1958

7. *A. R. Orage, a Memoir*, Phillip Mairet, 1936 (Introduction)

8. *New Age*, March 6, 1919 (Orage as R.H.C.)

9. *Caravansary and Conversation*, Richard Curle, 1937, p. 178

10. *Let there be Sculpture*, Jacob Epstein, 1955, pp. 59–61

11. Mairet, p. 41

12. *Letters*, p. 63

13. *Letters*, p. 344

14. *New Age*, June 1910, p. 182

15. *New Age*. Letter to Editor, E.P., August 18, 1910

16. *New Age*, August 1910, p. 373

17. To P.H., August 1953

18. To P.H. in conversation

Chapter Eight. Definitions

1. *A Retrospect*, *Lit. Essays*, p. 11

2. G. to K., p. 227

3. *The Oxford Book of Modern Verse*, Introduction by W. B. Yeats, 1935

4. *Egoist*, *Ezra Pound*, by Jean de Bosschère, January 1917, and sub.

5. *Letters*, p. 191

6. *Egoist*, de Bosschère, as above

7. *Future*, September 1917

8. *Egoist*, de Bosschère

9. *Mesmerism*, *Selected Poems*

10. *Make it New*, E.P., 1934, p. 81

11. *Lionel Johnson*, *Lit. Essays*, p. 367

12. *Exultations*, E.P., 1909

13. *The Poetry of Ezra Pound, The Pre-Imagist Stage*, N. Christoph de Nagy. The Cooper Monographs, 1960, p. 133

14. *Autobiographies*, W. B. Yeats, 1955, p. 461

15. *T.P.s Weekly*, June 1913

16. *Bookman*, March 1910

17. *English Review*, December 1909

18. *The Desirable Alien*, V. Hunt and F.M. Hueffer, 1913, p. 72
19. *Letters*, p. 224
20. *The Poetry of Ezra Pound*, Hugh Kenner includes a memo. by Ezra Pound, on 'This Hulme Business', p. 307
21. *New Freewoman*, December 15, 1913
22. *New Freewoman*, September 1, 1913
23. *Letters*, p. 35

24. *The Critical Attitude*, Hueffer, p. 94
25. *New Age. Osiris* series, December 7, 1911
26. *New Age. Osiris* series, December 21, 1911
27. See Canto 18, p. 87
28. *New Age. Osiris* series, January 25, 1912
29. *New Age. Osiris* series, February 15, 1912
30. *New Age*, December 21, 1911

Chapter Nine. Frith Street

1. *Letters*, p. 288
2. *Letters*, p. 292
3. To P.H., December 21, 1956
4. To P.H.
5. *T. E. Hulme*, Michael Roberts, 1938, p. 15
6. In talk with P.H.
7. *Blasting*, etc., Lewis, p. 112
8. In talk with P.H.
9. As above
10. *T. E. Hulme*, Roberts, p. 12
11. *Life and Opinions of Thomas Ernest Hulme*, A. R. Jones, 1960
12. *Life and Opinions of Thomas Ernest Hulme*, quoted from *New Age*, February 1909
13. *Egoist*, May 1, 1915

14. *Polite Essays*, E.P., 1937, p. 8
15. *The Poetry of Ezra Pound*, Hugh Kenner, 'This Hulme Business'
16. To P.H., November 17, 1957
17. To P.H., November 11, 1956
18. *The Honeysuckle and the Bee* J. C. Squire, 1937
19. To P.H., November 11, 1956
20. To P.H., June 6, 1957
21. *Let There be Sculpture*, Jacob Epstein, 1955, pp. 59–61

Chapter Ten. Holland Street

1. Remark made to P.H.
2. To P.H., April 7, 1954
3. To P.H., November 29, 1956
4. *Lit. Essays*, p. 8
5. *English Review*, *A Study of English Poetry*, Henry Newbolt, March to June, 1912

6. G. to K., p. 49
7. In conversation with P.H.
8. *The Poetry of Ezra Pound*, Kenner, 'This Hulme Business'
9. *Life for Life's Sake*, Richard Aldington, 1941, p. 134
10. To P.H., October 30, 1953
11. To P.H., December 1, 1953

12. To P.H., December 21, 1956
13. *Egoist*, June 1, 1914
14. *Poetry*, March 1913
15. *New Freewoman*, August 15, 1913
16. *Imagist Anthology*, edited Ford Madox Ford, 1931
17. *Make it New*, p. 335

Chapter Eleven. London and Away

1. *Lit. Essays*, p. 303
2. *Patria Mia*, 1962, p. 38
3. *Letters*, p. 43
4. *Patria Mia*, p. 9 and sub.
5. *Lit. Essays*, p. 334
6. *Patria Mia*, p. 35
7. To P.H., March 3, 1957
8. Canto 79, p. 520
9. Canto 74, p. 460
10. G. to K., p. 82
11. *Ancient Lights*, Hueffer, 1911, p. 235
12. *London Town Past and Present*, 1909. *On the Future of London*, Hueffer.
13. *Ancient Lights*, p. 268
14. *Ancient Lights*, p. 269
15. *English Review*, February and December 1911; March 1912
16. *New Age*, May 1911
17. *The Critical Attitude*, Hueffer, 1911, p. 9
18. *Poetry and the Modern Novel*, Compton Mackenzie, 1933
19. *Edward Marsh*, Christopher Hassall, 1959
20. Canto 74, p. 472
21. *Lit. Essays*, p. 214
22. *Patria Mia*, p. 68
23. *Roger Fry*, Virginia Woolf, 1940
24. *English Review*, March 1912
25. Canto 79, pp. 516 and 522
26. *English Review*, August 1911, p. 167
27. *English Review*, January 1912

Chapter Twelve. Innovations

1. *New Age, Through Alien Eyes*, E.P., January 30, 1913
2. *Life for Life's Sake*, Richard Aldington, 1941
3. *Autobiography*, John Cournos, New York, 1935
4. *New Age*, Editorial, January 1914
5. *New Age, Through Alien Eyes*, E.P., January 13, 1913
6. *New Age*, letter by Arthur Thorn, November 23, 1911
7. *Lit. Essays*, p. 9
8. *Selected Poems*
9. Canto 76, p. 486
10. Canto 74, p. 453
11. T. Parkinson in *Yeats and Pound, Comparative Literature*, Oregon, vol. 6, no. 3, 1954, from an unpublished letter by E.P. in Yale University Library
12. W. B. Yeats, B.B.C. broadcast, 1936
13. *Autobiographies*, Yeats, p. 493
14. *Poetry*, April 1914

Notes

15. *Poetry, Status Rerum*, E.P., January 1913

16. Quoted by Harriet Monroe in *A Poet's Life*, U.S.A., 1938, p. 267

17. To P.H. on tss., 1961

18. *W. B. Yeats*, J. M. Hone

19. *Letters of W. B. Yeats*

20. Mrs. W. B. Yeats in conversation with P.H.

21. *Letters*, p. 52

22. *Ripostes*, E.P., 1912, Introduction

23. '*Phasellus Ille*', *Selected Poems*

24. *Egoist*, Webster Ford, E.P., January 1, 1915

25. *New Age*, January 6, 1910, p. 253; *New Poems*, William Watson, 1909

26. *Egoist*, Ezra Pound, de Bosschère, January 1917

27. *Egoist, Poetry, a Magazine of Verse*, E.P., June 1, 1914

28. *Letters*, p. 43

29. *Letters*, p. 44

30. *Letters*, p. 47

31. *Salutation, Selected Poems*

32. For final version see *Selected Poems*

33. *Selected Poems*

34. *Egoist*, de Bosschère

35. *Poetry*, February 1913

36. *Selected Poems*

Postscript

1 *Poetry*, June 1915

Index

Abbey Players, at Court Theatre, London, 1909, 84; at Yeats's home, Woburn Buildings, 87

Abbott, Ella, of Holland Street restaurant, 134, 135

A.B.C. teashop, Chancery Lane, 107, 108

'Absolute rhythm', 131

Addison, Joseph, at Holland House, 72

'A Few Don'ts by an Imagiste' (E.P.), 136

Agadir incident, 143

Aldington, Richard: at Church Walk, 69; description of eyes, 70; contributes to *New Age*, 104, 108; and Imagism, 134; and *Poetry*, 156; on Pound in 1912, 149–50

Alexander, Cecily ('Harmony in Grey and Green', Whistler), 71n.

A Lume Spento (E.P.), 47, 48, 57, 58, 63n., 84; T. S. Eliot comments on, 58

Ames, Professor, 37

Ardnagashel, County Cork, 16

Astafieva, Serafima, teacher of ballet, 148

Aubrey House, Kensington, 71

'Aunt Hebe' ('Aunt Frank') in Canto LXXXIV, 41

'Ballad of the Goodly Fere' (E.P.), 55, 107, 114, 144

Barham and Marriage, grocers, Church Street, 68

Baryatinskaya, Princess, 141, 141n.

Barrie, James, *What Every Woman Knows*, 80; Mrs. James, 72

Barzun, Henri-Martin, at Church Walk, 69

Beddoes, Thomas Lovell, E.P.'s appreciation of, 112

Bedford, Agnes, 69

Beerbohm, Max, *Zuleika Dobson*, 143

Belloc, Hilaire, 149; as progressivist, 106; in *New Age*, 104; *The Servile State*, 106

Bennett, Arnold, 108, 149; in *New Age*, 104

Billy, André, *Époque 1900*, 23, 159

Binyon, Laurence, 59; introduces E.P. to Wyndham Lewis, 92

Bishop, Daphne (Mrs. Clifford Bax), 57

Blunt, Wilfrid Scawen, 93, 111

Book of the Rhymers' Club, The, 58

de Born, Bertrans, 56

Bosnia and Herzegovina, Austria annexes, 1908, 95

Bottome, Phyllis, 61; on Pound's parents, 28

Boyle, Robert, at Holland House, 72

Bridges, Robert, as innovator, 132

Brontë, Charlotte, visits Thackeray in Kensington, 71

Brook Green, Pound moves to, 57

Brooke, Rupert: and Edward Marsh, 144; at a Frith Street gathering, 144–6

Brown, Ford Madox, 53

Brown, Ivor, contributes to *New Age*, 104, 108

Browning, Robert, Pound on, 63, 81, 112, 141; Ernest Rhys and, 93; Rhymers' Club and, 111

Burckhardt, Jacob, *The Civilization of the Renaissance*, 119, 119n.

Burgos, Pound describes, 39

Bynner, Witter, arranges for American publication of *Provença*, 77

171

Index

Café Royal, 129

Camden Group, 129

Camoens, 76

Campbell, Joseph, 32, 128

Cannan, Gilbert, 72

Cannell, Skip, at Church Walk, 69

Cantos (E.P.), 13, 16, 20; references to themes and individuals in: 'Aunt Frank', 41; Binyon, 92; 'donative' writers, 120, 120n.; Cunningham Grahame, 73; Italian visit, 1911, 152; Colonel Jackson, 27; James Joyce's Jesuit education, 44n.; King Menelik, 121, 121n.; Leighton House visit, 72; Wyndham Lewis, 92; Professor Emil Levy, 43; Pope Pius XI, in Milan, 44; H. Spencer, 32; Swinburne, 60–1; Thaddeus Pound, 31n.; Venice, 45; Vienna Café, 92; Yeats at Woburn Buildings, 86

Canzoni (E.P.) printed in London, 1911, 77; Pound on criticisms of, 78; and the *Georgian Anthology*, 144

Carlyle, Thomas, *The French Revolution*, 71

'Cathay' (E.P.), 159

Catullus, Imagists' appreciation of, 136

Cavalcanti, Guido, Pound's renderings of, 78–9

Chalais, 43

Chateaubriand, in Kensington Gardens, 72

Cheltenham High School, Elkins Park, 33

Chesterton, G. K., 149; attacks on party system, etc., 106; on changed subject-matter of poetry, 126; on Orage, 104, 105; at the Poets' Club, 127; founds 'The Square', 61

Child, Professor, 37

Churchill, Winston, 144

'Civet Cat, The', Church Street, Kensington, 68

Cole, G. D. H., *The World of Labour*, 106

Colum, Padraic, 128

Conrad, Joseph, 149; in London, early century, 52, 54; in Holland Park Avenue, 89; on the Ford–Violet Hunt situation, 91; in first number of *English Review*, 88, 103

'Contemporeana' (E.P.), 157

Cooper, Fenimore, at Holland House, 72

Cooper, Gladys, 80

Cournos, John, 70n., 94, 150

Cowes, Pound visits, 41

Craig, Gordon: on Russian ballet, 148; *Art of the Theatre*, 148

Crawfordsville, *see* Indiana.

Curle, Richard, describes Orage, 105

Cursitor Street, 102–9

Damrosch's orchestra in Europe, 135

Daniel, Arnaut, *canzoni* of, 43, 44, 56, 77; Pound's renderings of, 77, 78; Pound on qualities of, 81, 82; as rediscoverer of style, 120

Dante: debt of, to medieval predecessors, 42; Pound translates, 77; debt of, to Arnaut Daniel, 81; Pound influenced by, 112

Darwin, Charles, *On the Origin of Species*, 110

De Bosschère, Jean, writes portrait of Pound, 1917, 112; on *Ripostes*, 156

Debussy, Pound on, 131

De Elizondo, Padre Jose Maria, 76

De la Mare, Walter, at 'The Square', 61; in *English Review*, 89

De Maetzu, on Orage, 105

De Maria's restaurant, Church Street, 134

De Stael, Mme, at Holland House, 72

Diaghilev, 148

Divus, Andreas, translates *Odyssey* into Latin, 38

'Donative' writers, 120

Doolittle, Hilda, 'H.D.', in student days, 35–6; at Church Walk, 69; in London, 130; as Imagist, 134, 135; and *Poetry*, 156

Dorothy Plaisance restaurant, Holland Street, 134, 135

Index

Doughty, Ford on, 118

Douglas, Norman, in *English Review*, 89

Dowson, Ernest, 87, 93, 113

Draft of XXX Cantos (1933), 17

Du Bellay, Joachim, Pound translates, 77

Duchess Street, Langham Place, Pound in, 49

Dukes, Ashley, 128

Dumas, A., Pound's early reading of, 31

Edinburgh, possible visit of Pound to, 38

Edward VII, death of, 98

Egoist, The, Pound writes in, 157

Eliot, T. S., 17; *The Waste Land*, 13; on Pound as teacher, 15; and present book, 18; on *A Lume Spento*, 58

Elkin Mathews' bookshop, Vigo Street, 58, 59, 60; *and see* Mathews

Ellis, Havelock, 81; the attitude to his *Psychology of Sex*, 81

Elsie, Lily, 80

English Review, The, 56, 59, 61, 62, 154; on Pound's *Spirit of Romance*, 77; Ford as founder of, 88; first number of, 88; Sickert writing in, 148; on the Russian ballet, 148; described, 88 seqq.; new editor of, 102, 142; on Bergson, 143

Epstein, J., at Frith Street, 129; and Hulme, 125

Ervine, St. John, contributes to *New Age*, 104

Evening Standard, 56, 58

Exultations (E.P.), 113; reviews of, 114; quoted, 115–16, 152

Fabian Arts Group, 104

Fabian Society, 98

Farr, Florence, 69; music for poetry by, 84–5, 94; introduces Pound to Poet's Club, 128

Fenollosa, Ernest, 157

Figgis, Darrell, on Pound's poetry, 107

Finnegan's Wake, 18

Fitzgerald, Desmond, 17, 17n.; introduces Pound to Poet's Club, 128

Fitzroy Square home of Ford Madox Ford, 53

Fletcher, J. G., 69

Flint, F. S., 56; at Church Walk, 68, 69; on Pound, 94, 114; in *English Review*, 89; on Imagism as a joke, 135–6; on *Ripostes*, 155; on Hulme, 125; in Poets' Club, 126–7; *The Net of the Stars*, 114; reviews *Personae*, etc., in *New Age*, 103; reviews *Canzoni*, 1911, 77–8; in *New Age*, 62, 103

Flynn, Mr., of Philadelphia Mint, 31

Ford, Ford Madox, 49, 50, 51, 52; Pound first meets, 59; education of, 54; collaborates with Conrad, 54; his value to Pound, 54; poetic role of, 132; and Violet Hunt, 90–1; tries to obtain a divorce in Germany, 114; finds a room for Pound, 57; and Swinburne, 60; at 'The Square', 61; at Church Walk, 69; in Sussex, 71; as Pound's guide to London, 72; at 84 Holland Park Avenue, 89 seqq.; introduces D. H. Lawrence to Ernest Rhys, 94; in 1908, on probable war with Germany, 95; on the Boer War, 141–2; on Imagists, 137; on Meredith's death, 61; on perils and potentialities of change, 142, 143, 144; on the poet's duty, 117, 118, 119; on Pound's 'unintelligibility', 118; on Ruskin's influence on Hunt, 69; on Yeats, 85; Pound on method of, 21, 116; Read on, 55; Wells on, 54; Wyndham Lewis on, 91; 'Canzone a la Sonata' (E.P.), 122–3; *The Critical Attitude*, 117; 'High Germany', 116, 122–3; 'The Poet's Eye' in *The New Freewoman*, 117; *The Pre-Raphaelite Brotherhood*, 52; *The Spirit of the People*, 53

Forster, E. M., *Howard's End*, 143

Fowler, Arthur, 121n.

France, Anatole, Pound on, 131

Frazer, Sir James, *The Golden Bough*, 84, 95

Freud, Sigmund, 81

Index

Frith Street circle, 124–9, 144, 146

Frobenius, Leo, 17n.

Frost, Robert, at Church Walk, 70; *A Boy's Will*, Pound reviews, 31–2

Fry, Roger, 146

Furnival, Professor, 80

Gallup, Donald, *A Bibliography of Ezra Pound*, 59

Galsworthy, John: at 'The Square', 61; in *English Review*, 89; Ford meets Violet Hunt at house of, 91

Garnett, Edward, 149

Gaudier-Brzeska, 69, 112, 146

Gaunt, William, *Kensington*, 72n.

George V, accession of, 98

George Leib Harrison Foundation scholarship, 38

George, W. L., 69

Georgian Anthology, 144

Gerrard's *Herball*, 94, 94n.

Gibraltar, Pound in, 42

Gibson, Wilfred, at Frith Street, 146

Giessen, 114, 117

Gill, Eric, at Second Post-Impressionist Exhibition, 1912, 146

Glengarriff, County Cork, in War I, 16

Goldring, Douglas, 89; *South Lodge*, 90, 91

Concourts, the, Pound cites, 21

Goslings, of Regent Street, 129

Gosse, Sir Edmund, 149; suggests Poets' Club, 126; at Yeats' Woburn Buildings home, 87; Pound's opinion of, 111, 117

Gourmont, Remy de, Pound's interest in, 151

'Grace Before Song' (Pound), 63

Grafton Gallery, 146

Graham, Cunninghame, 73; at Holland Park Avenue, 91

Gregory family, of Coole Park, Galway, 26

Gregory, Horace, on Pound's grandfather, 26

Gregory, Lady, 154; Yeats describes Pound to, 1909, 84

Guide to Kulchur (Pound), quoted, 17n., 38–9

Guild socialism, birth of, 106

Hailey, Idaho, the Homer Pounds in, 27

Hamilton College, Clinton, New York, Pound at, 36, 37

Hamilton Literary Magazine, Pound's first published poem in, 37

Hamlet, incest theme in, 80

Hampstead, 93, 94

Hardy, Thomas, 52, 91; Ford on, 118; 'A Sunday Morning Tragedy', 88

Harrison, Austin, editor of *English Review*, 142, 143

Harwell, F. S. Flint in, 135–6

Hastings, Beatrice, as 'Professedly Gorged Saynsberrie' in *The New Age*, 106–7

'Hawkesby, Mrs.', 141

Heine, Pound translates, 77

Helston, John, *Aphrodite*, 70, 70n.

Hewlett, Maurice, 52, 60, 141; as innovator, 132

Heyman, Katherine, American pianist, 48, 59, 69

'High Germany' (Ford Madox Ford), 116, 122

Hirschfeld, Dr., *Intermediate Sexual Types*, 81

'Histrion' (E.P.), 113, 115–16

Hobson, S. G., on workers' partnership in industry, 106

Holborn Empire, 108

Holland House, 72, 72n.

Hone, Joseph, on Yeats' liking for Pound, 85

Hopkins, G. M., 111

Horace Mann High School, New York, William Carlos Williams at, 34

'How I Began' (series in *T.P.'s Weekly*), 55

Hueffer, Ford Madox, *see* Ford, Ford Madox; the change of name, 53

Hueffer, Dr. Franz, Ford Madox Ford's father, 52–3; on Rossetti, 54; *The Troubadours: a History of Provençal*

Index

Life and Literature in the Middle Ages, 53

Hudson, W. E., 88, 91, 93–4

Hueffer, Oliver, eldest son of Franz, 53

'Hugh Selwyn Mauberley' (E.P.), 159

Hulme, T. E., 20, 56, 116, 146; dinner circle of, 22, 105; described, 125; on honest poetry, 126; Epstein on, 129; Epstein's bust of, 125; and Imagism, 133–4; and Edward Marsh, 144; poems of, in *Ripostes*, 155; and Pound, 124–9

Hunt, Violet, 69, 89–90; autobiography and novels of, 90; and the women's suffrage movement, 96; at Giessen with Ford, 114; *The Desirable Alien*, 114–15

Hunt, William Henry, watercolour painter, 69, 69n., 89; Mrs. W. H. Hunt (novelist), 89

Hutchins, Patricia, on James Joyce, 14n.

Huxley, Aldous, 17

Huxley, T. H., *Zoological Evidence of Man's Place in Nature*, 110

Hyde, d'Orsey, 69

Ibsen's *Ghosts*, a reading of, 87

Idaho, the Homer Pounds in, 27, 38

'I gather the limbs of Osiris' (E.P.), 119

Illustrated Woman's Magazine, The, 80

Image, Selwyn, 59

Imagism, 124, 133–7; Pound's definition of, 136–7; Yeats on, 153; precision of, 154; Amy Lowell and, 137

Indiana, Pound teaching in, 39, 44, 45

'Indiscretions' (E.P.), 25, 25n.

'In Durance' (E.P.), 39

Ionides, Alexander, 111

Ionides. Luke, *Memoirs*, 111, 111n.

Irving, Washington, at Holland House, 72

Islington, Pound moves to, 56–7

Isle of Wight, the young Pound visits, 41

'I Vecchi' (E.P.), 111n.,

Jackson, Col., in the *Cantos*, 27, 111, 111n.

Jackson, Holbrook, 104

James, Henry, 13, 45, 47, 149; Pound on method of, 21, 136, 140, 141; Pound on *The American Scene* of, 29–30; contributes to first number of *English Review*, 88, 103; in America, 1908–11, 140; remonstrates over talk, 91; on 'British Sundays', 59; *The American Scene*, 29–30, 138

James, Scott, on *A Lume Spento*, 58

James, William, 59, 140

Janus of Basel, Pound quotes, 65

Japanese Exhibition of 1910, Shepherd's Bush, 117

Jepson, Edgar, meets Pound at 'The Square', 61, 62

John, Augustus, Gordon Craig on, 148

Johnson, Lionel, 58, 93; Yeats on neglect of, 87

Joy, Mrs. E., of the 'Yorkshire Grey', 55

Joyce, James, 15, 18, 20, 23; in Canto XXXVIII, 44; *Chamber Music*, 58; *Portrait of the Artist as a Young Man*, 15

'Juno women', Pound describes, 80

'Just word' of Flaubert, 133

Kenner, Hugh, 57; re 'false starts' of *Canzoni*, 1911, 77

Kensington: Church Street, 14, 16; Church Walk, 66–74; Gardens, 73; Palace, 72–3; Square, 71; literary associations, 71, 72

Kepplewhite, Mrs. Ethel, 128

Kerr, Miss M. E. Granger, 49n., 57n.

Kinross, Albert?, 107

'La Fraisne' (E.P.), 47, 64

Lamb House, Rye, Henry James at, 140–1

Langley family, Church Walk, 68, 69, 70

'Langue d'Oc' (E.P.), 37

Lansbury, Lord (*The Herald*), 107

Lauder, Harry, 108

Law, Hugh, 94

Index

Lawrence, D. H., 17, 155; at Church Walk, 69; in *English Review*, 89; reads his poems to Ernest Rhys, 94; *The White Peacock*, 143

Leber's Restaurant, Holland Park Avenue, 111

Lechmere, Kate, 125, 126, 133–4

Leighton, Lord, Kensington house of, 72, 72n.

Leno, Dan, 80

Leopardi, Pound translates, 77

Letters of Ezra Pound (1950), 21–2

Levy, Professor Emil, 43–4

Lewis, Percy Wyndham, 18, 91–3; and Hulme, 125; at Second Post-Impressionist Exhibition, 146; contributes to *New Age*, 104

Literary Essays (Pound), 131n., 136n.

'Little Tich', 89

Lloyd George, David, historic budget of, 98

Lohr, Marie, 80

London's cultural rôle, early in the century, 47

Loomis family, 25–6

Lope de Vega, Pound's study of, 38, 49n., 76

Lowe, Lady, 105

Lowell, Amy, 137

Lustra (E.P.), 28, 158, 159

Macaulay, Lord, in Kensington, 71

McCarthy, Lillah, 80

MacDaniel, Professor, 37

Mackenzie, Compton, 143, 144

Macleod, Fiona, 113

Madrid, Pound studies in, 38

Mairet, P., on Orage, 105

Manning, Frederick, Australian poet, 76, 76n., 132; *Canzone* to Dorothy Shakespear, 76n.; *Scenes and Portraits*, 76n.

Mansfield, Katherine, contributes to *New Age*, 104, 108

Marlow, Louis, 130–1

Marsh, Edward: at Frith Street evening, 144–6; and the *Georgian Anthology*, 144

Marwood, Arthur: founder of *English Review*, 88; in John Doe scheme, 121

Masefield, John, 58; at 'The Square', 61

Masterman, C. F. G., *The Condition of England*, 1909, 99–100

Mathews, Elkin, 58, 59, 60, 61; and Swinburne, 61; publishes *Personae* and *Exultations*, 60, 61, 113

Mathews, Mrs. Elkin, 59, 60

Mathews, Nest, 59

Mead, G. R. S., *The Quest*, 84

Meredith, George, 52, 61

'Mesmerism' (E.P.), 113

Milan, Ambrosian Library, Pound studies in, 44

Mill, John Stuart, in Kensington Square, 71

Mirandola, Pound translates, 77

Mond, Sir Alfred, and *English Review*, 102

Monro, Alida, 130

Monro, Harold, opens Poetry Bookshop, 130

Monroe, Harriet, 138; founds *Poetry*, 156; Pound works with, 156–8

Moore, George, 52; contributes to *English Review*, 103

Moore, Mary, of Trenton, 36

Moore, P. Sturge, 93

Moore, Thomas, at Holland House, 72

Morris, William: Dr. Hueffer's friendship with, 53; Pound reads, 113; Ford's exasperation with, 118

Murry, Middleton, at Frith Street, 146

de Nagy, Christoph, on Pound's poetry, 113

National Guilds League founded, 1915, 106

Nevinson, H. W. (*Daily News*) at 'The Square', 61; at Frith Street, 146

New Age, The, 25n., 95, 99, 126; Flint reviews *Personae* in, 62; Pound writes to, on religion, 84; 'Patria Mia' (E.P.) first appears in, 138n.;

Index

'Money Changers in Literature', (E.P.) in, 143; on London poverty, 150

Newbolt, Henry, 58; as joint president of Poets' Club, 126; *A New Study of English Poetry*, 132-3

New English Weekly born, 1932, 106

New Freewoman, The, 117, 136

New Magazine, The, 1909, 80

Newton, Isaac, in Kensington, 71

'New York' (E.P.), 139n.

Nicolson, Harold, on Edward VII's reign, 98, 99

'Night Litany, The' (E.P.), 55

Nineteenth Century and After, Pound writes in, 117

Norman, Charles, 26

Notting Hill Gate (the 'Gravel Pits'), 71

Ogontz, Pennsylvania, 32

'Old English Rose' restaurant, Holland Street, 134, 135

'Old Sceptre' Chop House, 129

Orage, A. R., editor of *The New Age*, 103, 156; Pound on, 103-4; 105; various descriptions of, 105; and Major C. H. Douglas, 104, 106

'Paideuma' (Pound on Frobenius' concept), 17n.

Paris, early visit to by Pound, 38, 41

'Passionate Cino' (E.P.), 43

Pater, Walter, 72

Patmore, Brigit, at Church Walk, 69, 70

'Patria Mia' (E.P.), 138n., 140

Pavannes and Divagations (E.P.), 26, 27

Pennefather, the Rev. R. E., 82, 83

Pennsylvania, University of, 33, 37-8, Yeats lectures at, 1906, 84

Penty, Arthur J., *Restoration of the Guild System*, 104

Personae (E.P.), 52, 60, 61, 128; Dedication of, 36; Yeats praises, 84; Flint reviews in *New Age*, 62-3; Pound on his objects in, 101n.; 'To Whistler, American' in, 140n.

Philadelphia Mint, 30

Philippe, Jean, of Church Walk, 66, 68

'Piccadilly' (*Personae*), 52

Pisan Cantos (E.P.), 21, 32, 74; Henry James in, 141

Pisanello, 151

Pius XI, Pope, at Milan Library, 44

Plarr, Victor, 59, 93

'Plotinus' (E.P.), 113, 115

Poe, E. A., Eliot on, 13

Poetry: founded, 156; Fenollosa's work in, 157; H.D.'s Imagist poems in, 135; Yeats' poems in, 154; Pound's comments on Yeats in, 153

Poetry and Drama: birth of Imagism mentioned in, 134

Poetry Bookshop, Devonshire Street, 130

Poetry Review (later *Poetry and Drama*), 130; Pound's 'credo' in, 131

Poets' Club, founding of, 126; Chesterton and Shaw at, 127

Polytechnic, Regent Street, Pound lectures at, 1909, 75

Post - Impressionism, 136; Virginia Woolf on, 146

Pound, family of: Thaddeus Coleman, Ezra's grandfather, 26, 27; in *Canto* XXII, 31; Homer Loomis, son of Thaddeus, father of Ezra, 26, 27, 33; becomes assayer in U.S. Mint, 29, 30; a 1928 interview with, 75; Mrs. Pound, his wife, William Carlos Williams describes, 35

Pound, Dorothy, 33n., 57n.; *see also* Shakespear, Dorothy.

Pound, Ezra (chronological): family background, 24-36; birth of, 27; in Great Blizzard of 1887, 28-9; the move to Wisconsin, 29; to Philadelphia, 29-30; early visits abroad with Aunt Frank, 40-2; visits London Mint, with father, 33; student days, 33-6; first published poem of, 37; later studies at Pennsylvania, 37-8; in Europe in, 1906, 38; studying in Spain, 38; teaching in Indiana, 39-40; sets out for Provence,

Index

Pound, Ezra (*contd.*)

42; in Venice, 44, 45; first collection of poems published, 45–6; in London, 1908, 47–74; at Church Walk, 66–74; London life, 75–87; changes of address, 48–9, 55, 56–7; lecturing at Regent Street Polytechnic, 75; at work on *The Spirit of Romance*, 76 seqq.; and Imagism, 124–37; at Giessen, 114–15; in America, summer of 1910, 138–40; at Oxford and Cambridge, 146; summary of influences on, 110–14; in Paris, Italy, 1911, 151; on 'absolute rhythm', 131; on business of poet, 78–81, 120–4, 131–7; on 'Celticism', 113; on his early work, 32; on expatriates, 139; on London's 'literary institutions', 149; on religious ideas, 83, 84; on materialism and crime, 107; on 19th century generally, 110–11; on Russian ballet, 148; on 'symptomatic' and 'donative' writers, 120; on universities, 37, 110; on want, 150, 151; on Epstein, 129; on Ford's criticism, 116, 117, 154; on D. H. Lawrence, 155; on Swinburne, 60, 110; on Turner, 69; on Yeats, 152–4; publications, *see named entries, also* 'Notes', for shorter pieces, and *Cantos, Exultations, Literary Essays, Pavannes, Personae, Pisan Cantos, Ripostes, Selected Poems*; in *English Review*, 89 seqq., 103; in *New Age*, 84, 103–9, 119; in *New English Weekly*, 103–9; in *Poetry Review*, 131; and Cournos, 150; and Hilda Doolittle, 35–6 (*in each case, see these names separately*); and Major Douglas, 106; and T. E. Hulme, 124–9, 133; and Henry James, 140, 141; and E. Jepson, 62; and Edward Marsh, 144, 146; and H. Monroe, 156–8; and Quiller-Couch, 156; and Ernest Rhys, 94; and Edward Thomas, 62; and W. Carlos Williams, 33–6, 86–7; and Wyndham

Lewis, 92–3; and W. B. Yeats, 84–5, 153, 154; described as 'cryptosemite', 92

Pre-Raphaelites, as 'an industry', 110

Propertius, Pound translates, 77

Proust, Marcel, 20, 143

Provença (E.P.), 77

Provence, 42 seqq.

'Provincia Deserta' (E.P.), 43

Psychology, new interest in, 80

Quest, The (publ. G. R. S. Mead), 84

Quiller-Couch, Sir Arthur, 156

'Quinzaine for This Yule, A', (E.P.), 59

Read, Herbert: contributes to *New Age*, 104; on Ford, 55

'Revolt against the crepuscular spirit in modern poetry' (E.P.), 65

Reynolds, Stephen, *A Poor Man's House*, 91

Rhymers' Club, 93, 153

Fhys, Ernest: editor of 'Everyman', 59; encourages Pound to write *Spirit of Romance*, 76; at Holland Park Avenue, 93

Rhys, Grace, 93

Richard of St. Victor, 77

Richardson, Dorothy, quoted, 86

Ripostes (E.P.), 134, 139n., 155, 156

Rizzio murder, 38

Roberts, Michael, on Hulme, 125, 126

Robey, George, 108

Ross, Robert, 127

Rossetti, Christina, Violet Hunt sends poems to, 90

Rossetti, D. G., 63, 78–9, 89, 110

Rossetti, William, and Ford Madox Brown, 53

Rothenstein, William, 85

Round Pond, the, 73, 109

Rowan Road, Hammersmith, 49n.

Rummel, Walter, 151

Ruskin, John, the Hunts and, 90

'Russettings', Chorley Wood, the Elkin Mathews' home, 59

Index

Russian ballet, 148

Rye, Henry James at, 140, 141

Saintsbury, Professor George, 117

St. Mary Abbot's church, 66, 70, 82, 83

San Pietro in Mavino, 151

San Zeno, church of, Verona, 151

Sappho, Imagists' appreciation of, 136

Schelling, Professor, 37–8, 119

Schopenhauer, Franz Hueffer as pupil of, 53

Scott, Sir Walter, Pound's early reading of, 30, 31

Selver, Paul, at Church Walk, 69

Sestina Altaforte (E.P.), 56, 129

Seymour, Ralph Fletcher, Chicago publisher, 70

Shakespear, Dorothy (Mrs. Ezra Pound), 75, 77

Shakespear, Olivia, 75, 77; writes down Luke Ionides' *Memoirs*, 111n.; with Dorothy, and Ezra Pound: visits Yeats, 87; in Italy, 151

Shepard, Professor William, influences Pound, 37, 76

Shepherd's Bush Empire, 89

Sickert, Walter, on Post-Impressionism, 146–8; contributes to *New Age* 104

Sidney's 'Astrophel and Stella', 133

Simpson, Henry (Poets' Club), 126, 127

Sinclair, May, 59

Sirmione, 151, 152

Sitwell, Edith, in *New Age*, 104

Sloninsky, at Church Walk, 70, 70n.

Smith, William Brooke, 47–8

'Snapdragon' (D. H. Lawrence), 155

Social credit (Major Douglas's), 104n., 106

Sonnets and Ballate of Guido Cavalcanti (E.P.), 78

Sordello, Milan Ambrosian Library, accounts of, 44

South Lodge, Violet Hunt's home, 89; *see* Goldring

Spain, Pound studies in, 38, 39, 76

Spectator: free verse and strict scansion controversy in, 131

Spencer, H. (Cheltenham Military Academy), 32

Spencer, Stanley, in 1912, 146

'Square Club', 61, 62

Squire, J. C., on Frith Street group, 128

Storer, Edward, 127, 129

Suffragette movement, 90, 96, 142

Swift, Stephen, & Co. (publishers), 78

Swinburne, A. C., 52, 113; Pound on importance of, 63, 110; Rhymers' Club on, 111; circle of acquaintances of, 61; at 'The Pines', 60; death of, 61

Symons, Arthur, 52; *The Romantic Movement in English Poetry*, 143; *Wanderers*, 113

'Symptomatic' writing, 120

Synge, John, 21, 58, 84, 153

Tagore, Rabindranath, 149; and *Poetry*, 156; Yeats and, 85

Talleyrand in Kensington, 72

Tancred, F. W., Pound describes, 128; and Hulme, 127, 128

Tempest, Marie, 80

Tennyson, Alfred Lord, 111, 118; Pound on, 156, 156n.

Thackeray: in Kensington, 71; *The Newcomes*, 53

'The Condolence' (E.P.), 158

'The Eyes' (E.P.), 120

'The Needle' (E.P.), 155

'The Rest' (E.P.), 158

'The Return' (E.P.), 100–1, 154

'The Seafarer' (E.P.), 155

'The Virginal' (E.P.), 155

'The White Stag' (E.P.), 63

Thomas, Edward: praises early work of Pound, 62; at Holland Park Avenue, 91

Thompson, Francis, Pound's opinion of, 63, 146

Thorn, Arthur, 107, 108, 151

Tilley, Vesta, 80

Times Literary Supplement, 64, 78–9

'To Whistler, American' (*Personae*, E.P.), 140, 140n., 158

179

Index

Tolstoy, L., in first number of *English Review*, 88

Tour Eiffel restaurant, Soho, 128, 129

Tristram Shandy quoted, 28

Troubadours, 76, 82; *see* Provence

'Turkish Coffee' café, Soho, 55

Umbra (E.P.), 63n.

United Arts Club, St. James's Street, 126

Upward, Allen, 99

Venice, Pound's visits to, 44, 45

Verhaeren, E. de, 150

Verona, 77

Victoria, Vesta, 89

Vienna Café, near British Museum, 56, 92

Villon, François, 76, 118; Imagists' appreciation of, 136

Wabash College, Crawfordsville, Indiana, 39, 44, 45

Wadsworth, Joseph, linking Weston and Longfellow families, 26; at Frith Street, 146

Walpole, Horace, at Holland House, 72

Washington, D.C., 18; Pound's work in, 21

Watson, William, 155–6

Watts-Dunton, Theodore, 60–1

Weaver, Harriet Shaw, on Pound, 23; visits Yeats with Pound, 85–6

Wells, H. G., and *English Review*, 88, 91; influence of, 99; and *New Age*, 104; on Ford-Conrad collaboration, 54

West, Rebecca, defends Imagists, 136

Weston family, 26; Miss Weston, marries Homer Pound, 27; her father and mother (E.P.'s grandparents), 28, 30

Weygandt, Professor, 38

Whistler, James, 13; 1912 Loan Exhibition of works of, 140; 'To Whistler, American' (E.P.), 140, 140n., 158

'White Heather' restaurant, Holland Street, 134, 135

Whitman, Walt, in London, 47; and Pound, 113, 113n.

Wilde, Oscar, 52, 127

Wilkinson, Mr., *see* Marlow, Louis

Williams, William Carlos, 22, 33–6, 116; as doctor and writer, 34; Pound advises, 39–40, 60, 63; at Church Walk, 86–7; on *A Lume Spento*, 48

Withey, Mrs. (Duchess Street), 48, 55

Woburn Buildings, home of W. B. Yeats in, 44, 85, 154

Woolf, Virginia: on Post-Impressionists, 1910, 146; on O. W. Holmes, in *Times Literary Supplement*, 64; on American art and politics, 64

Wordsworth, William, at Holland House, 72

Wright, the Rev. Charles, 18

Wyncote, Pennsylvania (Phil), 29, 31, 33

Yavorska, Lydia, 141n.

Yeats, J. B., 59

Yeats, W. B., 20, 23, 26, 34, 52, 72, 85, 86, 87, 90, 149; in America, lecturing, 84; in *English Review*, 89; Figgis on, 107; Ford on, 118; on Imagists, 153; poetic admirations of, in youth, 111; and *Poetry*, 154, 156; Pound's appreciation of, 34, 152, 153; his admiration of Pound, 63, 84, 85, 154; on rhetoric in poetry, 132, 153; visits Rhys, 94; and the Shakespears, 75; *Autobiographies*, 114; *Celtic Twilight*, 65; *Wind Among the Reeds*, 58

Yellow Book, The, 58